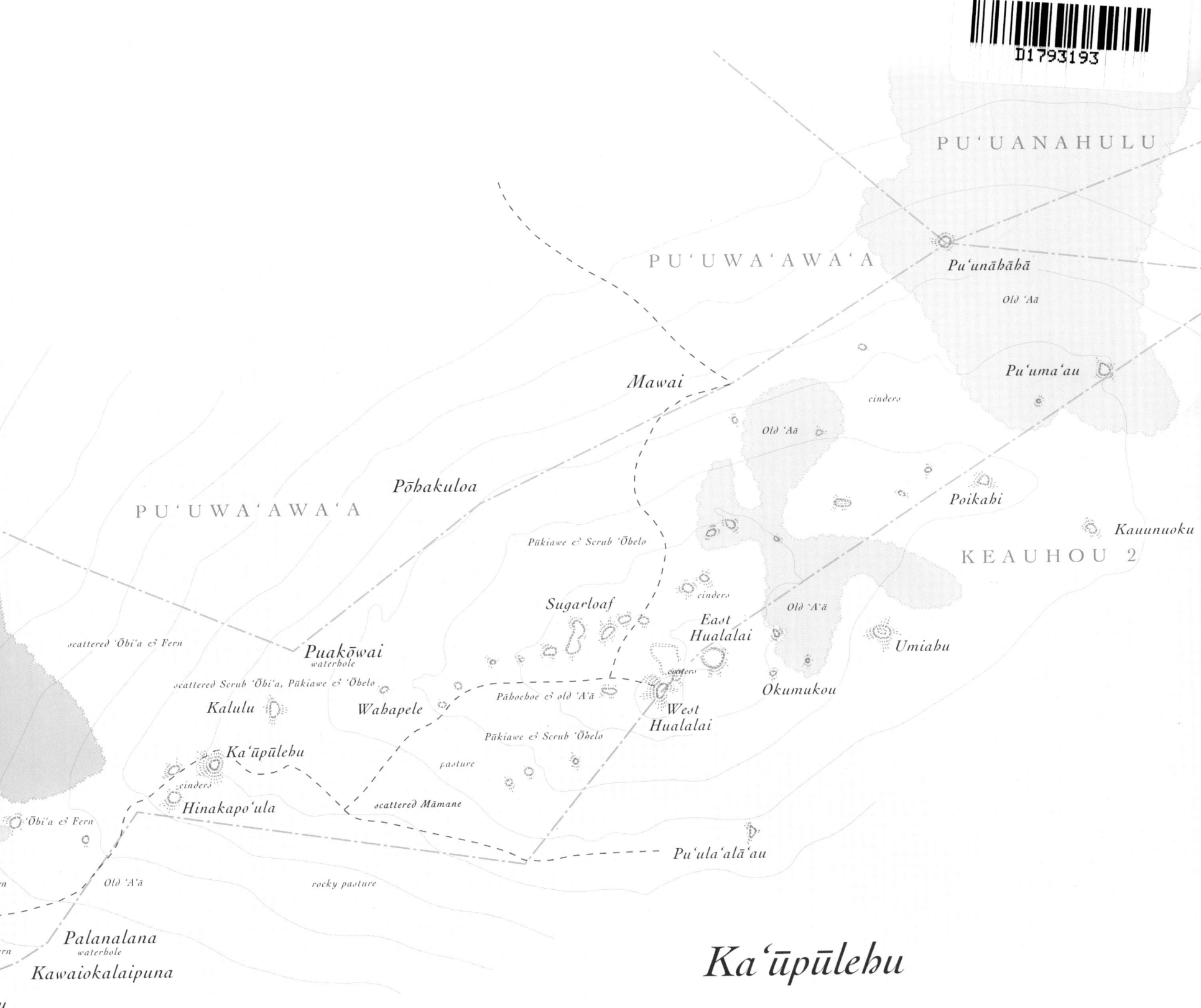

# Ka'ūpūlehu

Hawaiian place names that are verifiable have been included with the appropriate diacritical marks (glottals and macrons) on this historic rendition of the region. Names that are no longer in use, or whose meanings could not be ascertained, appear without diacriticals. Place names have been reviewed by Hawaiian language scholar Larry Kimura.

*In the Lee of*
# Hualalai
*Historic Kaʻūpūlehu*

# *E Kū*
O Kū

# *E Kāne*
O Kāne

# *E Lono*
O Lono

*Hualalai's presence sweeps through Kekaha from a summit 8,271 feet high in the rarefied* wao akua, *the distant mountain region believed to be inhabited by the gods and spirits. As Hualalai's cones, craters, and* puʻu *tumble to the sea, the cloud and dryland forests move one into the other, above to below, boundary to boundary. At the shoreline, anchialine ponds mirror the past and the parched* ʻaʻā *and* pāhoehoe *reach to contain the ocean.*

*Kuʻua mai i ke ola*
Let down the gift of life

*I nā pōmaikaʻi*
And all the blessings with it

*A ea ka lani*
Till the heavens

*ka honua*
and earth be heaped

*Ea iā Kāne-*
Let them be raised by

*i-ka-wai-ola*
Kāne of the living waters

*E ola mai kahi*
May there be life from one

*pae a kahi pae*
boundary to the other

*E ola mai luna a lalo*
From above to below

*Mai kaupoku*
From roof

*a ke kahua—*
to foundation

*E ola—*
  May there be life—

*a ola loa no*
  Everlasting life

*Opening prayer from The Polynesian Family System in Ka-'u, Hawai'i, by E. S. Craighill Handy and Mary Kawena Pukui.*

*In the Lee of*

# Huala

# LAI

## Historic Ka'ūpūlehu

**JOCELYN FUJII**

*Photography by*
**FRANCO SALMOIRAGHI**

*Introduction by*
Hannah Kihalani Springer

# Contents

*Introduction 1*

Place of Power
*8*

Pele's Wrath
*42*

Blood and Bureaucracy
*62*

Astride on the Kaha Lands
*82*

New Horizons
*104*

*Lava Flows Map 114*

*Notes 115*

*Glossary 116*

*Bibliography 118*

*Acknowledgments 120*

*Index 121*

*Aloha mai kakou.*

*'O au no he kaikamahine o ka
   mauna ki'eki'e o Kona,*

*'O Hualalai ka inoa.*

*'O au no ka pulapula o na pulapula
   o ka 'āina kaulana o Hualalai,*

*'O Kekaha ka inoa.*

*'O au no ke kama o ko makou
   'āina aloha ma Kekaha.*

*'O Kukui'ohiwai ka inoa.*

*Aia 'o Kukui'ohiwai ma Ka'ūpūlehu.*

*E kipa mai kakou ia Ka'ūpūlehu,
   ia Kekaha, ia Hualalai.*

*E kipa mai kakou i ko makou 'āina aloha.*

*Aloha mai.*

Aloha.
I am a daughter of Hualalai,
the lofty mountain of Kona.
I am the offspring of the
offspring of Kekaha,
a celebrated region of Hualalai.
I am a child of our beloved
homeland at Kekaha,
Kukui'ohiwai is its name.
Kukui'ohiwai is located
at Ka'ūpūlehu.
Welcome to Ka'ūpūlehu,
to Kekaha, to Hualalai.
Welcome to our
beloved homeland.
Aloha.

*Hannah Kihalani Springer, whose children are the fourth generation to live at Kukui'ohiwai in the uplands of Hu'ehu'e, pauses at the family cemetery at a hill called 'Akahipu'u.*

*Overleaf — Revered for its crystalline waters and shade-giving* kou *trees, the shoreline pond called Luahinewai reflects Hualalai's splendor.*

HUALALAI. Before I knew its name, I knew its bulk beneath my feet, I knew its rhythms by my family's activities, I knew the view from it, across not-so-wide seas, to not-so-distant islands. While its true loft rose up, distant behind our home, Kukui-'ohiwai, the hills and plains and points and bays of the region of Kekaha spread out, seemingly near, below. My childhood impression was that the lava hills and channels of Ka'ūpūlehu were the source of the entire landscape seen from home.

I now know Hualalai's name and it is still that which bears my weight. Our family's activities are still tied to the rhythms of its mass. When rains fall, our water tanks are replenished, allowing shamelessly long showers. During dry times, we do not need to weed our flower beds or mow our lawn because vegetative growth comes to a virtual standstill. If fire rages across its flanks, we cringe in anticipation of newly configured plant communities and reduced native plant cover. During certain months we look forward to plump reef fish for eating, such as *kole*, during others to humpback whales cavorting in the seas between not-so-distant islands, during others to the showy and sweet fruit of the *ēlama* tree, and so on throughout the year.

The lofty height of the mountain is not so distant now. With the benefit of four-wheel-drive transportation and generous neighbors, our family is able to access those remarkable places that comprise the cloud forests and subalpine plains as well as the quietude of the summit itself.

But it remains the lava lands and shoreline of that part of North Kona known as Kekaha that I first see upon arising in the morning and that I drink in with each sunset view. These are the land forms which are etched indelibly in my mind...the curves, the swells, the flats, the points, the cracks, and channels that the volcano formed.

That volcano, Hualalai, fed the island to form our homeland and seems to have been terrifically active in our home *ahupuaʻa*—traditional Hawaiian land division—of Kaʻūpūlehu. The last eruptive episodes of Hualalai occurred at sources along the northeast and southwest borders of the *ahupuaʻa*. And so my childhood hyperbole was just that, an exaggerated truth: the lava hills and channels of Kaʻūpūlehu are responsible for most of what I see before me.

An ordered relationship has been established for you with regard to the landscape: the mountain, Hualalai, may be subdivided into regions such as Kekaha, and Kekaha, in turn, subdivided into *ahupuaʻa* such as Kaʻūpūlehu. And it is at Kaʻūpūlehu that our home, Kukuiʻohiwai, as well as your destination, is located.

There is also order to my relationship to these places, and that, too, has been established for you. I am a daughter of Hualalai, an offspring of offspring of Kekaha, a child of Kaʻūpūlehu. For us of Hawaiʻi, this is more than metaphor, it is deep genealogy. It establishes our place in the litany of occupants of the land, our place in the continuum of changing land uses and changing human values.

In Kaʻūpūlehu, as anywhere else, change is a source of challenge, if not outright conflict, for us who are of the land. Our family, living in the land of our ancestors, has not embraced the frenetic pace of transient American society. We do not measure our success by movement away from the family homeland, but rather by our ability to stay in it.

And this is a challenge.

*A portrait of Luka Hopulaʻau, Hannah Springer's great-great grandmother and the first wife of John Avery Maguire, the founder of Huʻehuʻe Ranch, graces the living room of Kukuiʻohiwai.* Courtesy of Hannah Kihalani Springer.

As a child, I learned a story of mischievous *menehune* who desired to gain renown for prodigious earth-moving activity. With supernatural powers, they desired to move the top off of one *puʻu* located upon the mid-slope of Hualalai and to place it atop another *puʻu* located by the sea. Each time they were about to accomplish their task, a higher power intervened and thwarted their efforts. They finally tired of the effort and abandoned their endeavor.

This myth offers a mighty metaphor for the prodigious earth-moving activity that goes on in Kekaha today. With seemingly supernatural powers, capital and influence move across oceans, continents, and islands in the way that the *menehune* used to move across the flanks of Hualalai. *Puʻu* and lava fields are

*Seen from the uplands of Huʻehuʻe, the clouds above the Kaʻūpūlehu shoreline speak a language all their own.*

reconfigured with ease, and though there has yet to be intervention of a higher power, that is not to say that we do not await it. That is not to say that it will not come.

Intervention of higher powers fills the mythic reality of Kaʻūpūlehu. As a child, I learned of the time when drought came to the land and the crops failed and the people came close to death. Kāne, the patron of fresh water, came among the stricken people and showed them fresh water to be harvested from the sea. I accept Kāne as the mythic source of the water. I also accept the real ingenuity of my ancestors to tap the freshwater springs which flow into the ocean.

Perhaps the most powerful metaphor comes from the "historic" 1801 volcanic eruption of Hualalai. This eruptive episode formed the lava delta upon which the Keāhole Airport is situated today. Beneath this place where trans-Pacific travelers now arrive and depart, the great fishpond of Pāʻaiea once thrived. The source of this eruption, the *puʻu* known as Puhiapele, is located where the breadfruit grove of Kāmehaʻikana once was.

According to the myth, Pele, the patron of the volcano, visited destruction upon these important aquacultural and agricultural resources because the great chief, Kamehameha, had failed to honor her sufficiently. And so the lava flowed from Kaʻūpūlehu south and west across Kekaha.

According to our history, our social, political, and economic systems were still healthy and vital enough in 1801, that Kamehameha caused his forces to be mobilized and their

*From left, Hannah Kihalani Springer, Eva Kameleapililua Dayton, and Springer's children, Thelma Kihalani Tomich and Kekaulike Prosper Tomich, place a lei at Kūki'o in remembrance of a beloved friend and teacher, Lani Stemmermann.*

efforts to be focused at nearby Kīholo, where another fishpond was built. This pond was described by the English missionary, William Ellis, as being 600 acres in size. In 1859 a mighty Mauna Loa eruption flowed across Puʻuanahulu and into Puʻuwaʻawaʻa and covered the Kīholo pond. In 1859 our society was in the throes of transition and distracted to the extent that no new pond was built.

There are those who say that this is a metaphor for the loss of health and vitality of the Hawaiian people. There are those who liken the intrusion of foreign ways to the lava flows covering the landscape. But perhaps they go too far, too fast. Perhaps we are as a people where Kamehameha was in 1801, regrouping and marshaling our forces to replace great loss through constructive effort.

I, for one, have realized the loss of familiarity with my home landscape. Places I believed to be parts of my birthright have been gouged and disfigured, claimed and populated, rendered unfamiliar and crowded. I have been, according to mood and time of the moon, angry and discontented, lamenting my sense of loss to any and all within earshot. I have been dreamy-eyed with what might have been and what might yet come to be. I am now committed to taking action toward realizing the dream of what might yet come to pass. I am prepared for constructive effort.

I spend my days learning the myths and the parts of our history which I have yet to learn. I cross-reference them, the fanciful with the geological, the cultural with the biological, the legendary with the historic. I spend my days sharing these impressions and insights with our children and with our friends, through the spoken and written media. I share these things with college students and with visitors, and, as with my earlier angst, I share with any and all within "earshot."

And as I delve into our history and discuss it with my peers, truths of the deep culture of our people are clarified for me. Our culture is one which has valued compatibility rather than domination, collectivism rather than individualism, and inclusion rather than exclusion.

As I apply these values to our Hawaiian history, I realize that the newcomers, by virtue of their arrival to my *ʻāina hānau*, have become a part of the history of the *kamaʻāina* and are now a part of my genealogy. As inclusive as this is, the implied intimacy goes hand-in-hand with deeper scrutiny. We want and expect those who enter our family to come with sincerity and humility, we want our relationship to be imbued with propriety, we anticipate causes for joy and for pride, and we know the potential for disappointment.

So here you have it before you, a book prepared with sincerity and humility, with as much propriety as could be mustered. It is an effort that I hope has brought as much joy to the other participants as it has to me. The words, the images, the design, and the intent cause me to have pride in the wonders of my homeland and the ingenuity of my people. The newcomers' chapters in history are still being written. The burden is upon them not to disappoint.

*Hannah Kihalani Springer*
*Kukuiʻohiwai, Kaʻūpūlehu, Hawaiʻi*
*April 1995*

*Place of Power*

Overleaf—*Viewed from Nawahine at the summit area of Hualalai, Mauna Kea emerges from the clouds.*

*Just beyond the northern boundary of Kekaha is 'Anaeho'omalu's Ku'uali'i, one of the major fishponds on Hawai'i island. Maintained until the 1960s, it was a thriving source of stock for other ponds in the region, as well as for fish for many a ranch lū'au.*

*The mountain's* mana *extends from summit to sea, where even the rolling* ʻiliʻili *submerged in the ocean have their source in Hualalai. Once a part of the lava flow that reached the shore, the submerged* pōhaku, *photographed at a* hālau waʻa *(canoe house) near a* kīpuka *called Waiulu, lend sound and dimension to the Kaʻūpūlehu shoreline.*

EVEN TODAY, Hualalai speaks. The primal powers that have shaped the land still resonate through the landscape, through the leeward plains and anchialine ponds, the dry and cloud forests, the velvety *puʻu* and rolling flanks of this mighty mountain of Kona.

Hualalai, the mother of Kona. Hawaiian mythology refers to Hualalai as the fertile wife of the mariner Hawaiʻi-loa, who sails from the Marquesas Islands to this land of *ʻawa* and coconuts. From Hualalai and Hawaiʻi-loa spring the people of Hawaiʻi and the districts of Hawaiʻi island. One of those districts is Hāmākua, the name of Hualalai's last child. When Hualalai is buried, it is on the great mountain of Hawaiʻi that bears her name today.

From a summit named Hainoa, some 8,271 feet high, the slopes of the mountain tumble to the sea, cradling the boundaries of North Kona, one of the eight districts of Hawaiʻi island. Within North Kona is the region of Kekaha, bordered by the sea, Honokōhau to the south, ʻAnaehoʻomalu to the north, and Nāpuʻu—the hills of Puʻuwaʻawaʻa and Puʻuanahulu—in the uplands. *Kekaha Wai ʻole*, it is called: the waterless Kekaha of the Kona district, where water is valued as wealth.

Without water but laden with other riches, the lands of Kekaha have been prized from the beginning. In Kekaha, in the shelter of the three great mountains of Hualalai, Mauna Kea, and Mauna Loa, have walked kings and chiefs, farmers and fisherfolk, hardy ranchers, and seaworthy villagers. Battles have been won and lost here, villages have thrived and vanished, legends have been born and shattered. Throughout the centuries, through the turbulence of eruptions, droughts, wars, and powerful natural phenomena, Hualalai, the sheltering mountain, endures.

Her slopes ascend gradually, as if poured to earth from a tear in the sky. Her internal rumblings are felt in the lifeways and rhythms of the region, and in the ringing silence of the summit area. The wind is her breath, swirling across the hills and plains. She is old but she is young, the third youngest of the five volcanoes of Hawai'i island. She cradles, yet is herself cradled—to the northeast by Mauna Kea, to the south and east by Mauna Loa. Far north are the Kohala Mountains, the oldest on the island, and beyond Mauna Loa to the southeast, the young and feisty Kīlauea.

On this land of volcanoes, the terrain was shaped by lava, claimed by lava, created and destroyed by lava. Smooth, ribbony, fast-moving *pāhoehoe* and the slow, crumbly *'a'ā* coursed down Hualalai's slopes in 1800 and 1801, and down Mauna Loa in 1859, rearranging the landscape each time. "It is no wonder that the simple fisherfolks living along the sea-coast personified the Volcano as a dreadful being with supernatural powers whose wrath bore down on them so much destruction, laying waste their gardens, and filling their fish-ponds with rocks, leaving them on a narrow strip of beach, the ocean on one side, and the lava fields on the other," wrote Eliza D. Maguire in her introduction to the 1926 edition of *Kona Legends,* a rich and evocative compilation. Lava represented the thirst, hunger, and revenge of the volcano goddess Pele as she poured her fiery tongues down the mountain, proclaiming her ascendancy over all who walked the land.

While many saw Pele as the ultimate architect of the landscape, the Hawaiians devised their own worldly system of land management. One division in that system is the *ahupua'a,* a section of land moving from mountain to sea, marked in the old days by a heap

*Overleaf—Crowned by a white rainbow, the summits of Mauna Kea in the distant left, Mauna Loa in the distant right, and Hualalai, where this picture was taken, converge in a saddle in the heights of the island. This rare configuration of summits places Hualalai in the lee of the other two mountains, the tallest peaks in the world when measured from their ocean base.*

*It is said that the gods Kū and Hina, to whom the ancients appealed for bounty in fishing, farming, and longevity, dwelled in the summit crater, Hainoa, near this cloud-misted area of Nawahine.*

of stones, an *ahu,* upon which the likeness of a pig—*pua'a*—or a pig itself had been placed as an offering, usually as a tax to the appointed overseer of the region, the *konohiki.* Ka'ūpūlehu, rich in lore, natural features, and plant and sea resources, is one of two dozen *ahupua'a* in the region of Kekaha, reaching from the shoreline upland in a wide wedge, past the summit of Hualalai, into the saddle where it meets the 13,679-foot-high Mauna Loa. From that rarefied summit area, where the mighty triad of Hualalai, Mauna Kea, and Mauna Loa converges, even the summit of Haleakalā is visible, brooding and magnificent on Maui, rising above the clouds on a clear day.

Here is the realm of the gods, where history and myth mingle and the deeds of the deities are larger than life. It is said that Hualalai's summit crater, Hainoa, was the ancestral home of the earliest gods, Kū and his wife Hina, to whom the Hawaiians appealed for bountiful harvests, success in fishing, and the assurance of future generations. These vast lands of Kona are also the realm of Lono, the god of agriculture and rainfall, whom the Hawaiians honored yearly with the *Makahiki* festival of harvest and thanksgiving.

Their ancient echoes still whisper through the dry and cloud forests that ripple through the land from summit to sea. In these upper reaches of the *ahupua'a* of Ka'ūpūlehu in the region of Kekaha, there are reservoirs and taro gardens, rich deposits of fine volcanic glass, sprawling ranch lands, and rare native vegetation—*'iliahi* (sandalwood), *'ōhi'a, 'a'ali'i, pūkiawe,* and *māmane*—which grow like shrubs at higher elevations. Looking down from this lofty crater, one can see fingers of black, gray,

A gnarly native ʻōhiʻa, unusually tall in the subalpine habitat where native plants tend to grow like dwarfs, towers above the shrub land in the upper reaches of Hualalai, some 8,000 feet above sea level. Hawaiians valued this tree for its roots, used in the construction of canoes, its sturdy wood, fashioned into idols and implements, and its flowers, sacred to the volcano goddess, Pele.

*The first man killed in battle was called a* lehua, *after this blood-colored blossom of the* ʻōhiʻa *tree. Because plucking Pele's favorite flower is thought to bring rain, the Hawaiians customarily pick* lehua *only when descending from a mountain. This dryland forest* lehua, *like the leaves and trunk of the tree, differs in appearance at various elevations. In the uplands, bird hunters looked for* lehua *as a marker for native birds, which fed on its nectar.*

*Near the Kipaheʻe cabin in the summit area of Hualalai, a venerable old* ʻōhiʻa *recalls the god Kū, whose name means "upright" and who occasionally assumed the form of the* ʻōhiʻa.

and brown lava reaching for the sea, punctuated with dimples, craters, spatter cones, small gullies, and assorted *puʻu*: greened over, or tawny with fountain grass, or untouched in their primal brown. Hidden in lava blisters and lava tubes are untold ancient burials. *Kīpuka,* islands of verdure or old lava spared by the most recent lava flow, can be seen at ʻOwēʻowē, at the border of Kaʻūpūlehu and Puʻuwaʻawaʻa in the uplands, and at Waiulu at the seashore, near a tiny black-pebbled bay that forms a natural canoe landing. In dark patches of green along the coast, wetland bird sanctuaries and anchialine ponds red with *ʻōpaeʻula,* tiny red shrimp used as fishing bait, still thrive among ghosts of the past. This broad view from mountain to sea is a blueprint of creation, of the lava flows and forces that have shaped the region in the last two centuries and beyond. Where the lava meets the ocean, waves crash upon natural depressions, and salt is made. Myriad hues of blue and black shimmer in the sunlight, deepened and textured by the rich reefs and offshore fishing grounds that have sustained upland and lowland dwellers since the beginnings of civilization in North Kona.

This is Kaʻūpūlehu: a model of efficiency in traditional Hawaiian land use practices, an *ahupuaʻa* marked even today by coastal and *ma uka–ma kai* (mountain-to-sea) trails that remind us of the resourcefulness of the region's inhabitants. In a rhythm of harvest and exchange up, down, and across the *ahupuaʻa,* the people of the seacoast gathered fish, dried and salted it with their harvests from the salt flats of Kalaemanō, wove *lau hala* baskets out of pandanus leaves, then exchanged them for the sturdy hardwoods, taro, and feather and plant resources of the uplands. And so it went, the rhythmic trafficking of food and materials up and down the slopes of Hualalai and up, down, and across the lands of Kekaha, on paths built stone by stone and navigated in the blistering heat, or by moonlight.

"The contrast between upland and lowland...was recognized economically in the distribution of land, each family receiving a strip at the shore and a patch in the uplands," wrote Martha Beckwith in *Hawaiian Mythology*. "It was recognized in the division of the calendar into days, months, and seasons, when those at the shore watched for indications of the ripening season in the uplands and those living inland marked the time for fishing and surfing at the shore."

*Ola akula ka ʻāina kaha, ua pua ka lehua i kai,* the Hawaiian proverb goes. "Life has come to the kaha lands for the lehua blossoms are seen at sea." J.W.H. Isaac Kihe, the renowned historian of Kekaha in the early 1900s who has been extensively translated by cultural resources specialist Kepā Maly, likened the people of the uplands to the *lehua* blossoms that blanketed their region in earlier times. "When the season arrived for deep-sea fishing," Kihe wrote in *Ka Hoku o Hawaii* in 1928, "many of the ma uka dwellers of Kekaha (the kaha lands) temporarily moved to the coastal villages. There their fishing canoes were seen coming and going, like lehua blossoms upon the sea."

ʻUmialiloa, the famed farmer, fisherman, and celebrated chief who united Hawaiʻi island in the 1600s, eight generations before the time of Kamehameha I, frequented the Kekaha shoreline in his fishing exploits.

*The* ma uka-*to-*ma kai *Makalawena trail, a government road established during the Kingdom of Hawaiʻi in the nineteenth century and still visible in North Kona, is an important legacy of previous generations. A major component of the coastal economy, trails connected the thriving fishing villages with upland dwellers, enabling them to exchange food and resources well into the ranching era.*

"Aku fishing was his favorite occupation," wrote the esteemed nineteenth-century historian Samuel Kamakau in his book *Ruling Chiefs of Hawaii*, "and it often took him to the beaches from Kalahuipuʻaʻa to Makaula."

Nor did Kamehameha I make any secret of his fondness for the Kekaha shoreline. The paramount chief of Hawaiʻi island, he lived from the mid-eighteenth century to 1819 and was the sole ruler to gain dominion over all of the Hawaiian Islands. "Fishing was the occupation of Kamehameha's old age at Kailua," wrote Kamakau. "He would often go out with his fishermen to Kekaha off Kaʻelehuluhulu and when there had been a great catch of aku or ʻahi fish he would give it away to the chiefs and people, the cultivators and canoe makers.... Kamehameha made a crafty bargain with the cultivators to give a single fish for a single bundle of pounded taro (paʻiʻai) or a calabash of poi, and so on...." In nearby Kailua and in Kekaha Wai ʻole—the waterless Kekaha—the most lavish gift one could offer Kamehameha was a simple cask of water.

When Kamehameha returned to Hawaiʻi island in 1812 following his conquests on Oʻahu, it was the lands of Kekaha that greeted him once again. The *aku* fleet—like *lehua* blossoms upon the sea—had been fishing since the early hours when Kamehameha's ship arrived at Kaʻelehuluhulu near Mahaiʻula Bay. In his account of the arrival in *Fragments of Hawaiian History*, the historian John Papa Iʻi wrote of the dazzling vision of the once-liquid and now-hardened *pāhoehoe*, as smooth and reflective as silver. "How beautiful that flowing water is!" Iʻi, then twelve years old, exclaimed from the ship. "Those who recognized it, however, said, 'That is not water, but pahoehoe. When the sun strikes it, it glistens, and you mistake it for water'."

That blinding image has changed little through the years, for *pāhoehoe* still covers vast tracts of land in Kekaha. The ranchers and fishermen who walked and rode horseback there in the nineteenth and twentieth centuries lived every moment of their lives on that lava. Countless times in their migrations they followed the fishing seasons, the wet and dry seasons, the seasons of harvest, carrying produce to the lowlands and fish to the uplands. "Most of the ocean living was seasonal," recalls Billy Paris, 72, a lifelong rancher and revered elder of Kekaha who managed Puʻuwaʻawaʻa Ranch from 1956 to 1959. "When school was out and the fish were running, even the kids would be out fishing and drying the fish." Upland dwellers, most of them affiliated with the early ranching communities of Huʻehuʻe and Puʻuwaʻawaʻa, would migrate to the sea carting stores of taro, sweet potatoes, pumpkins, and bananas. In those days, adds Paris, "Kaʻūpūlehu was more or less a fishing village, as was Makalawena. Makalawena at one time had a stable population, but my dad said that when he was young, it was a fishing village, close to the *aku* grounds. People would go fishing, dry their fish—*ʻōpelu, aku,* everything—and bring them up *ma uka* and sell them. They'd live at the ocean maybe three or four months of the year."

"Everything was fish," continues Joseph Makaʻai, who lived in Kaʻūpūlehu until he left at thirteen years of age, in 1931, to attend Konawaena High School. "*ʻŌpelu,* mullet, *akule.* In those days we had no time to run around and play. Everything was work,

work, work. Dry *'ōpelu*, go out fishing, dry *'ōpelu*, come back, clean the fish, salt." They salted the fish overnight, rinsed it off in the morning, and then dried it on the roof of the tool shed before the Chinese merchants arrived from the uplands to claim their seaside bounty. "They brought rice, flour, sugar," says Maka'ai. "In those days, a dollar bought 16 *'ōpelu* and my grandmother charged fifty cents for a *lau hala* hat. But what was money? Even if we had money, there was nothing to buy."

Maka'ai remembers growing taro, sweet potatoes, and pumpkins in small hills, called *pu'e*, that they tended carefully on the hill, Pu'u Mau'u, that served as their farming area more than two miles up the mountain. The two varieties of sweet potato, the yellow *huamoa* and the purple-skinned *hi'iaka*, grew well in the dry conditions, he says. The fruit of the *loulu* palm from the seaside was as close as they got to candy, except on those days when he could squirrel away a few pennies from the day's sale of *'ōpelu* for his favorite treat, the chewy red coconut candy purveyed by the Chinese merchants.

In this agricultural subsistence economy, so profound were the influences and uses of the land that they often defined a person's identity. Hannah Kihalani Springer, an ethnohistorian and descendant of the founders of Kekaha's renowned Hu'ehu'e Ranch, notes that it was customary for a resident of the *ahupua'a* to come forward and declare himself the son of a birdcatcher, imparting immediately the qualifications of his knowledge of the upper boundaries of the region. There, inhabitants hunted many of the prized birds—the now extinct *mamo* and *'ō'ō*, the

Loulu *palms still sway among the fishponds and legendary sites of Ka'ūpūlehu. In former times, villagers used their leaves as plaiting material and wall coverings, and their fruit for food.*

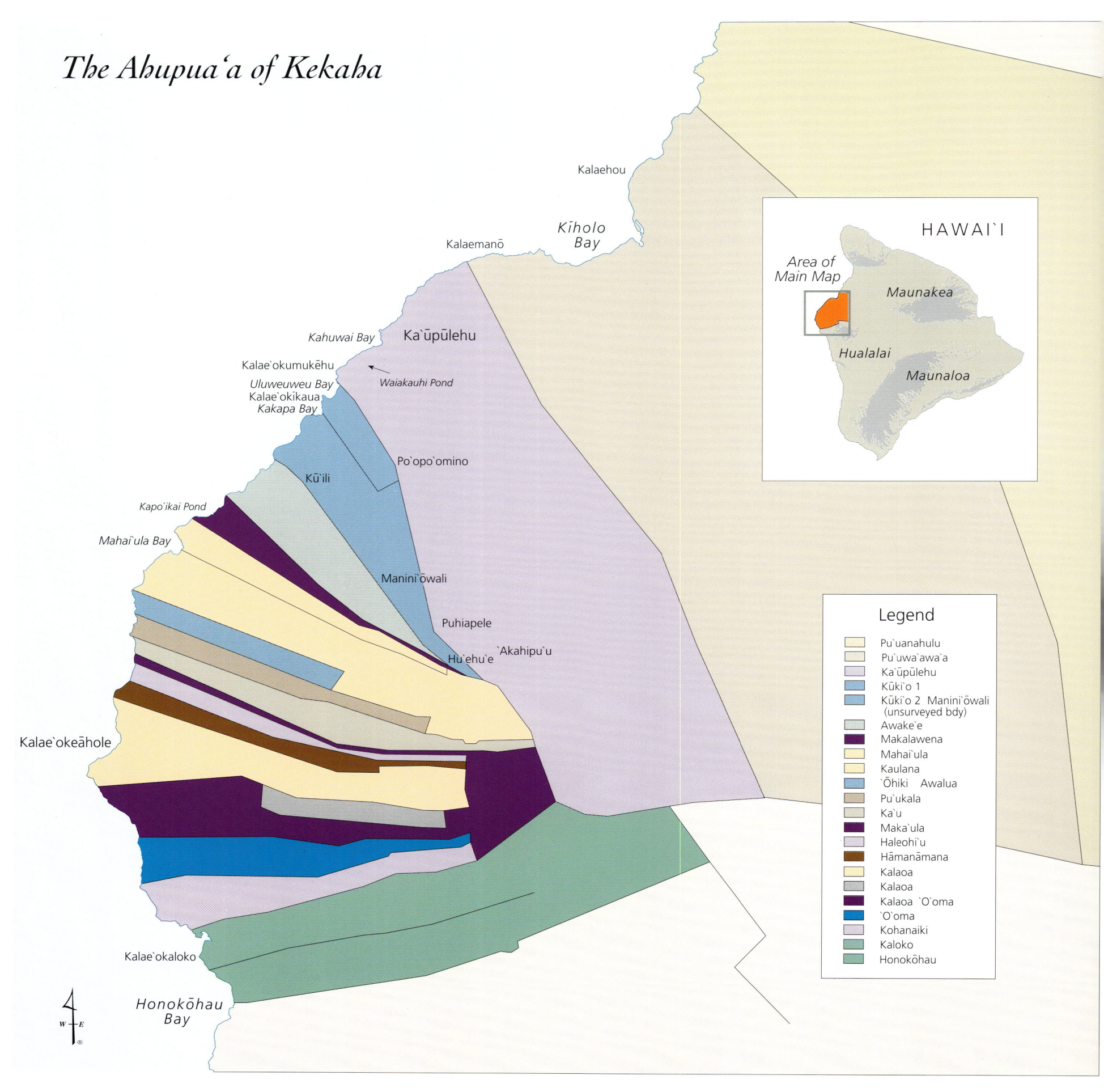

*The many* ahupuaʻa *of Kekaha reach from the mountain to the sea. Their boundaries form the basis of today's tax map system.*

rare *ʻiʻiwi* and *ʻapapane*—valued for the colorful feathers used to make the capes, helmets, and regalia of the *aliʻi* of old. According to Springer, in the years following the *Māhele* (Land Division) of 1848, when government lands were first made available for private land ownership, "bird hunters were very important resources in defining the landmarks of an *ahupuaʻa*." She says that in the upper regions of Kaʻūpūlehu, where the *ma uka* boundaries of the Honokōhau and Kaloko *ahupuaʻa* converge, claimants in the *Māhele* would note: "The land of Honokohau is where the old trees grow. That is where the *koa* [acacia, a prized native hardwood] is found. Kaloko is where the *ʻōhiā* grows—they are the younger trees." In 1873, during Commission of Boundaries hearings for the island, a resident had this to say about the markers of Makalawena, the most prominent seaside village in the early 1900s: "Thence turn ma kai to Hehapapawai, a small water hole in a small patch of pahoehoe boundary on [the] north side. Thence to the prickly pears growing on the aa and from thence the boundary strikes across the aa to Kukuinapuulehu aa. Thence ma kai to Pohakuanaiapoapu, a large round stone, thence to Moku pohaku on kohola, a large rock in the surf."

Lava flows served as important boundary markers, as at the *ahupuaʻa* of Kūkiʻo 1 and Kūkiʻo 2 at the shoreline, where the tall *ʻaʻā* flow met with the low *pāhoehoe* flow to form a line of demarcation. "It's important that we think of the *ahupuaʻa* as an economic unit, because oftentimes we see it as sort of an arbitrary line on the landscape," continues Springer. "Although this arbitrary line came from an earlier value and exchange system, the *ahupuaʻa* truly are the basis of our tax map system."

More than borders and boundaries, the *ahupuaʻa* system reflected the innate ability of Kekaha dwellers to read the landscape with an uncanny intimacy. Springer's ancestral homelands encompass the shoreline springs and bays of Kūkiʻo, the dryland forests sweeping upland, and the expansive plains and *puʻu* that ripple through the landscape from *ma uka* to *ma kai*—at their largest, some 24,000 acres of fee simple and 16,000 of leasehold land. A descendant of Kameʻeiamoku, a chief of Kaʻūpūlehu in the late 1700s, Springer traces her maternal and paternal lineage to Kekaha from the days before land ownership. Today she lives with her family some 1,800 feet high on the slopes of Hualalai, in a 100-year-old home called Kukuiʻohiwai in the lands of Huʻehuʻe, near where several of Kekaha's *ahupuaʻa* converge. It is a world of profound continuity in which the land is understood, its landscape read as a living language, its winds experienced as palpable breath, its seasonal scents anticipated. Springer's memories, warm and full of wisdom, encompass many generations of family and regional lore.

"Francis Iʻi Brown [one of Hawaiʻi's noted *kamaʻāina*] was an old family friend, and when I was a child, he was part of the reason I thought my mother knew magic," Springer recalls of the late Thelma Stillman. "Sheʻd be sitting up here at Kukuiʻohiwai and say, 'Oh! Uncle Francis must be going for *kole* now. Oh! Uncle Francis is fishing for *uhu* now'. Sheʻd say, 'If we go to town now, we can meet Uncle Francis's boat'. And we'd go to town and there would be Uncle Francis with *kole* and whatever other fish. I thought my mother possessed an awesome skill."

Springer watched her mother survey the landscape and seascape from their *lānai* at Kukui'ohiwai. She learned to see what her mother saw in the ocean far below: the distinctive wake formed by Brown's Hackercraft, barreling along beyond Ka'ūpūlehu, or Keawaiki, or Mahai'ula, and the spots where he anchored. "My mother knew where the fishing holes were because she'd gone fishing many times. She'd sit here and see the boat and know: that's a *kole* hole there, an *uhu* hole there, and that's what Uncle's catching. She also knew how long it would take for the boat to reach Kailua, so our rendezvous were perfectly timed."

Springer observes: "Growing up with someone who could see like that taught me that it's possible to know what is going on if you but look and develop the right interpretive skills. It is a skill that many of us are losing as we become immersed in the urban landscape."

As the elders holding those skills recede into history, people like Joe Maka'ai and his cousin, the late Robert Keakealani, who also grew up in Ka'ūpūlehu, take on a greater significance in the cultural integrity of the region. Maka'ai and Keakealani are among the last residents of the seaside village of Ka'ūpūlehu on the bay called Kahuwai (oldtimers like Maka'ai remember it as Kahuawai Bay), where the Kona Village Resort now stands. Their ancestors' bones lie hidden in burial caves there, and Maka'ai's family canoe, hand-hewn of precious *koa,* hangs from the rafters of the hotel's Hale Samoa dining room not far from where it was found.

"In the old days it was horseback or donkey—no cars," Maka'ai reflects as he gazes seaward from the Ka'ūpūlehu shoreline in 1994, the first time in many years that he had returned there from his present home in Hilo on the other side of the island. "And if you had to go in the ocean, you had to have a canoe. In those days, when you move, no car, no nothing, so how you going to carry a canoe? My grandfather just left it on the beach and that's where they found it when they came to build the hotel." The canoe lay on the beach for three decades, a ghost on the shore long after the villagers made their exodus to the uplands of Pu'uanahulu, or to Kailua. In the 1920s, only a dozen stalwart villagers remained at Kahuwai Bay, and by 1936, five years after Maka'ai moved away for good, the village was deserted.

Maka'ai's memories revolve around a life lived in austerity, yet imbued with a rich simplicity, a simple goodness. Fiber they picked from the trees protected them from the elements: *Pili* grass lined the exterior of the home, and his grandmother's handmade *lau hala* mats covered the interior walls and floors. Other homes were covered with the leaves of *loulu* palms, other roofs lined with coconut leaves. When Maka'ai was a child, there were only two or three families in the neighborhood.

In one of those families lived his cousin, Keakealani, a member of several generations of cowboys from the Pu'uwa'awa'a Ranch in Pu'uanahulu, born in Ka'ūpūlehu in 1916 and a renowned *paniolo* himself. When he died in 1990, Keakealani had been long gone from Ka'ūpūlehu, having left at twelve to work on the ranch in the uplands to help support his

*Joe Maka'ai at the shoreline of Ka'ūpūlehu, formerly a fishing village where he and his grandparents caught 'ōpelu for trade with the upland dwellers. A surviving inhabitant of the village, Maka'ai is an important resource for the region and a respected* kupuna, *a link to the ways of old.*

*The late Robert Keakealani, renowned for his skill in roping and a member of several generations of cowboys from Puʻuwaʻawaʻa Ranch, looks out over the hills he rode all his life. Keakealani, the father of the two sisters at left, knew every water hole, hill, cave, house site, and landmark in the area, and reminisced about the peaches and plums that grew bountifully in the uplands, as well as the fishing traditions of Kaʻūpūlehu, where he lived briefly.* Courtesy of Leinaʻala Lightner.

*Shirleyann Keakealani, left, and her sister, Leinaʻala Keakealani Lightner, stand before a stone wall that will one day encircle Lightner's three-acre home in Puʻuanahulu. Their grandparents used the same rocks to mark the boundary of their homestead, but the wall was displaced by a golf course. Relatives are moving the rocks, one by one, so a new wall can be built at Lightner's present home.*

siblings after their parents died. In 1972, when his daughter, Leinaʻala Lightner, began working at the Kona Village Resort, her father's memories came flooding back to him.

"We lived in the Puʻuanahulu homestead, and there were no roads down to this resort until the late sixties," explains Lightner, the resort's social director. "When I started working here, my father was thrilled because that meant he could come back home. When he'd visit, he'd show me all the places where Grandma would wash the clothes, where they'd get water from the spring, where they'd tie the donkeys, where they'd gather salt, dry the fish, gather ʻōpae." A large anchialine pond named Waiakauhi and other smaller ponds in the area teemed, as they still do, with ʻōpaeʻula, the red shrimp used as chum to attract the tasty ʻōpelu. Lightner's uncle, Joe Makaʻai, was taught to scoop the shrimp at night, by torch or lantern, when they swarmed to the surface of the pond and formed an easily captured layer of red. Once harvested from the ponds, the ʻōpaeʻula were bound into balls with dirt that was also painstakingly gathered.

To gather dirt to bind the ʻōpelu, Keakealani was taught to ride a donkey two miles uphill, to a cinder cone named Puʻu Nāhāhā. According to Lightner, "It was the only place that had dirt. There was no soil here. And it was dirt that could be packed into a mud ball." The fresh ʻōpaeʻula was mixed with the dirt or cinder, packed into balls, and paddled out in a canoe to the ʻōpelu fishing grounds, where it was released into the deep in the middle of a long, circular net. As the fishermen pulled up the nets, they were nearly blinded by the hefty numbers of wiggling, silvery fish that glistened in the sunlight.

Salt was a valuable trade item and essential for preserving the fish for the journey mai uka. For this, until as recently as the 1940s,

*When the heavens weep in the uplands, precious water percolates through the underground lava tubes to feed the anchialine ponds at the shoreline and these spring-laden waters of Kahuwai Bay. The beach rock prevents sea water and ground water from mixing freely. Waiokāne—the waters of Kāne—is a legendary spring that bubbles in the nearshore reefs of the bay.*

Kalaemanō, halfway between Kahuwai Bay and Kīholo Bay, and Waiaelepi near Kīholo, were the premier salt gathering spots. "It was a regular activity in my father's time," notes Lightner. "When the families came from *ma uka* or even as far away as Kohala to gather salt, they camped here three, four days, and sometimes they'd have hundreds of pounds of salt when they went home." To augment their supply, Lightner's grandparents made their own salt by putting pans of ocean water into the sun to dry. Makaʻai recalls using salt pans that he and his grandfather made out of coral limestone, which, until recently, remained visible at the shoreline fronting Kona Village.

"We used to harvest 300 bags in one season out at Kalaemanō," adds Robert Punihaole, a seventy-seven-year-old native of the region who came from a family of *paniolo* at Huʻehuʻe Ranch. "It was a lot of work, not just going over to pick up the salt. We used the puddles—tidepools—when they weren't filled up during the winter. We had to add water, let it sit a couple of days to dry on the rocks, add more water, stir it up, and dry it again, let it harden in the sun. That's how we made the salt grow. It was a hard procedure, but a lot of fun."

Punihaole was the one who buried his aunt, the legendary Annie Punihaole ʻUna, the last resident of the shoreline at Makalawena; she was renowned for her annual salt pilgrimages to Kalaemanō. "Among other things, she was famous for walking from her home at Makalawena to Kalaemanō for the best salt in the region," recalls Hannah Springer. "She made a seasonal harvest of it, in March, after the big winter surf and before the March rains." ʻUna and her second husband, Porto Alhambra, lived in the only home constructed in Makalawena after the 1946 tsunami.

The challenges of gathering drinking water were equally rigorous. A freshwater spring, Waiokāne—"the waters of Kāne," the god of creation in the Hawaiian pantheon—still bubbles out of the ocean at low tide in front of the Shipwreck Bar of the Kona Village Resort, recalling the days when it was a living faucet for the families of Kaʻūpūlehu. At low tide, residents brought an empty gourd stoppered with a finger, put it to the mouth of the spring, and filled it with its fresh and bountiful offerings. The custom succumbed to convenience in later years, when the gourds were replaced with gallon-sized soy sauce containers made of tin. Hannah Springer, who spent her childhood in the dry uplands of Huʻehuʻe and at spring-laden Kūkiʻo at the shoreline, recalls other ingenious methods her ancestors used, such as in Mākālei, a cave on a hill called ʻAkahi-puʻu that is celebrated in song and legend.

"During rains when water percolates beneath the earth, there are fantastic drips in the lava tubes," Springer explains. "The people of old would put hollowed-out log troughs, or *ʻumeke* [bowls], perhaps *ipu* [gourds], into the lava tubes and caves to collect the drip. In my great-grandparents' time, a redwood tank was assembled inside Mākālei to collect the water. This meant that during times of drought, the domestic needs of the residents were always met." The method, used well into the 1920s, also utilized vessels made of *koa*, *ʻōhiʻa*, and *kukui* wood, usually three to six feet deep. Land-clearing activities in the 1950s destroyed the cave's entrance. However, the drip method of collecting water was not unique to Kekaha but was an island-wide practice, explains Springer.

In another ingenious method, the Hawaiians tapped the interior walls of water caves to find the source of the moisture, then used stone tools to carve small irrigation troughs down the cave walls. According to Leinaʻala Lightner, the vertical troughs, like little flumes, caught the smaller drippings down the cave walls and directed them into a larger stream. Her father recalled that the method was used in the upland water caves. "Down at Kaʻūpūlehu, there's even a cave with stones that are waterworn," Lightner adds. "One large, flat stone is worn smooth by the water that flowed over it, and in another area, there are stone icicles that were formed by water."

"The interior of these caves was dark, so the Hawaiians used torches made of *kukui* nuts when collecting their water vessels," wrote E. S. Craighill Handy and Elizabeth Green Handy in *Native Planters in Old Hawaii*. "As troughs and other containers filled, water was dipped out slowly with a small coconut shell cup and poured into a gourd water bottle, using for a funnel the neck of another bottle gourd, cut off, or a ti leaf folded back on itself. The water was dipped carefully so as not to put sediment into the water bottle." Because the caves were considered sacred to the god Kāne, menstruating women were most unwelcome. Should such a woman enter, it was believed, the cave would dry up, requiring a formal exorcism by a *kahuna*, a priest. Offerings of pig and fish, taro tops, and an entire ʻ*awa* plant would be made amid elaborate prayer and ritual. Everything but the ʻ*awa* plant was cooked in the underground oven called an *imu*, then wrapped in *ti* leaves and placed near the cave's entrance. No one was allowed to enter during the *kapu* of ten days, proclaimed by a bundle of three bamboo stalks surrounded by a mound of grass. When the cave was reopened, it is said, the water flowed again.

"We had many such caves, such as Waikulukulu here in the Ahuaʻumi area of Hualalai, where the Hawaiians would put a calabash or wooden container to catch drip water," recalls Billy Paris, who knows Hualalai like his own backyard. "One day in the late 1970s, I was hunting up there and came across a wounded sheep. Right there was a cave that no one knew about. You could see rock underneath and it was covered with moss caused by the drip. There's another area where lava comes down near Puʻu O ʻIkaʻaka, and in that section of *pāhoehoe*, there's a stone that's been very carefully placed. Lift that up and there's water. It's hard now to find these places, because much of the vegetation and many of the trees that were used as landmarks no longer exist. But make no mistake, the Hawaiians knew where to find water in the mountains."

In 1992, in a two-mile lava tube about a mile above sea level at the hill called Puʻuwaʻawaʻa, biologist Jon G. Giffin discovered new and previously unknown species that had sought shelter and sustenance in Hualalai's subterranean world. In a tube estimated to be 3,600 years old, the bones of about thirty large, flightless geese were discovered, nearly twice as large as the native *nēnē*, with large leg bones to compensate for their modest wings. A smaller type of flightless bird, the Hawaiian rail, extinct since the 1800s, was also found, along with the bones of extinct native birds and those of sheep, goats, and other mammals.

*At the 2,500-foot level on Hualalai, volcanic nodules with a high olivine content form an otherworldly mound. The nodules, also called inclusions, were created by an eruption so rapid that it yielded large clumps of the green mineral, a geologic rarity.*

Particularly on this island, where the land is a vibrating mass of volcanic activity, the features of the land are temporal, altered by nature if not the human hand. "Hualalai is a living volcano," comments Hannah Springer. "For six months in 1929, our family was evacuated from our home because of a six-week episode when thousands of earthquakes shook the mountain. My mother and her sister described the great explosions they heard coming out of the depths of the mountain at night. They saw gas flames in the pastures behind the house. We had an intrusion, where magma emerges from great depths to the surface, close enough to expose a little gas, but not so close that the red hot lava of an eruption was visible."

While earthquakes rumbled through the mountains, storms, tsunamis, and the seasonal and climatic shifts of wind and water battered the shore. The awesome tsunami of 1946 decimated Makalawena's church, school, store, and the eight houses scattered around its precious anchialine ponds. It washed over the fishponds of Kīholo and left its mark on the underwater terrain of the bays, altering the general character of the Kekaha shoreline. Years later, as Leinaʻala Lightner sat with her father at the Kaʻūpūlehu shoreline in the 1970s, he recalled from his youth a poignant memory: the rustling, soothing sound of the surf as it washed over the *ʻiliʻili*—small black pebbles—in Kahuwai Bay.

"I told my father, 'There's no *ʻiliʻili* on the beach now'," she recalls. "'It's fine white sand'. And he said, 'In those days, there was *ʻiliʻili*.

33

*Kahuwai Bay, as photographed by Eliza Maguire in 1912, shows the starkness of a* pāhoehoe *landscape against a tranquil and barely peopled bay. The* kauhale—*group of homes*—*is where Joe Maka'ai, Robert Keakealani, and members of their family, the last residents of coastal Ka'ūpūlehu, lived.* Courtesy of the Kona Historical Society, from the Maguire-Stillman-Springer collection.

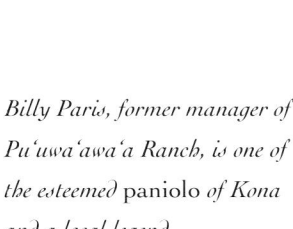

*Billy Paris, former manager of Pu'uwa'awa'a Ranch, is one of the esteemed* paniolo *of Kona and a local legend.*

Since the time when he was a child, there have been several tsunami disturbances that moved the rocks. That's why there's no *'ili'ili* on the beach anymore."

Lightner also remembers childhood camping trips at Kīholo Bay to the north, today a lagoon of black sand and pebbles. From Kīholo Bay south to Luahinewai, a distance of three-quarters of a mile, white sand lined the shoreline, she recalls. "The Kīholo lagoon was like a big turquoise swimming pool. It's not there anymore. The 1960 tsunami changed it into black sand. When we were children, we used to find Samoan crab, mullet, turtles. There are still a lot of turtles there, but other things have changed."

"Oh yes," confirms Billy Paris. "We have a picture of the lagoon at Kīholo before it was broken in half, when you just had a narrow entrance from the south side. It was a sanctuary for young fish in those days; the bay was alive. It was where the mullet used to come in and spawn. But the 1960 tsunami broke out the middle of the lagoon and since then, the tidal action has made a channel. At high tide the predators can get into the lagoon and clean out the smaller fish."

The echoes of the rustling *'ili'ili* on the shores of Kahuwai Bay still haunt Lightner, who imagines her father sitting at the shoreline in the days before concrete and jet aircraft, outdoors with his family enjoying dinner, the briny air on his face and the sounds of the waves in his youthful ears. "The rolling *'ili'ili*," she says. "He never forgot that sound."

More dramatic changes in the Kekaha landscape came from the opposite direction—*ma uka*. Eruptions from Hualalai in 1800–1801, possibly even in the late 1700s, and a mammoth flow from Mauna Loa in 1859, reassembled the terrain and enlivened the lore and legend of Kekaha. Two eruptive episodes in 1800–1801, called the Hu'ehu'e flow, pumped out large volumes of lava that

*Craggy Puhiapele presides over the lava delta that her prodigious eruption shaped some two centuries ago. Its lava, surging from below what is now the Māmalahoa Highway, merged with a flow from further upslope, above the highway in Huʻehuʻe.*

eventually covered a four-mile front at the seashore between Mahaiʻula and Keāhole Point, near where the Keāhole Airport stands today. The eruption was an awesome flexing of volcanic muscle by a modest, three-hundred-foot-high spatter cone called Puhiapele ("blown out by Pele"), visible just below the Māmalahoa Highway. From an elevation of 1,300 feet at Huʻehuʻe, on the northwest flank of Hualalai, its stark, angular profile still looms like a sentinel over the sprawling lavascape below.

Puhiapele's prodigious handiwork joined with the other Huʻehuʻe flow, originating in a cone above the highway, to cover two important economic resources: the breadfruit grove of Kāmehaʻikana in the uplands of Huʻehuʻe, and a fishpond at Pāʻaiea. At three miles long and a half-mile wide, the fishpond at Pāʻaiea was, according to Eliza Maguire in *Kona Legends*, so vast that it served as an inland waterway for canoes. "The fishermen going to Kailua and further south often took a shortcut by taking their canoes into the pond and going across, thus saving time and the hard labor of paddling against the ʻEka [a strong sea breeze from the south] and also the strong current from Keahole," she wrote. Recounting an eyewitness report of the eruption, William Ellis, who visited the island in 1824, wrote that the man "was astonished at the irresistible impetuosity of the torrent."

"The people believed that this earth-consuming flame came because of Pele's desire for awa fish from the fish ponds of Kiholo and Kaʻupulehu and aku fish from Kaʻelehuluhulu," wrote the historian Kamakau, "or because of her jealousy of Kamehameha's assuming wealth and honor for himself and giving her only those things which were worthless; or because of his refusing her the tabu breadfruit of Kāmehaʻikana, which grew in the uplands of Huʻehuʻe where the flow started." To appease Pele and save his fishpond, Kamehameha went by canoe to the lava front at Mahaiʻula and made an offering of pig and a lock of his own hair. "The flow had been destroying houses, toppling over coconut trees, filling fish ponds, and causing devastation everywhere," continued Kamakau. "Upon the arrival of Kamehameha and the seer and their offering of sacrifices and gifts, the flow ceased; the goddess had accepted the offering." Although Hualalai has been quiet since, scientists remind us that it is an active, not dormant, volcano.

Until recently, most accounts placed the Huʻehuʻe eruption at the same time—1800–1801—as the nearby Kaʻūpūlehu flow, which originated closer to the summit of Hualalai and was more prolonged and more complex, according to geologists. "The Huʻehuʻe flow could easily have been a six-month flow, but our guess is that the Kaʻūpūlehu flows may have lasted longer than that," explains David Clague, scientist-in-charge of the Hawaiian Volcano Observatory, an arm of the United States Geological Survey on Hawaiʻi island. "We're suspicious that the Kaʻūpūlehu flow dates not from 1800–1801, but from 1770 or 1780 or 1790. The Kaʻūpūlehu flow is clearly an eruption that lasted a long time." Like Kīlauea Volcano's thirteen-year, on-again, off-again activity, the Kaʻūpūlehu eruptions were possibly "episodic," according to Clague.

Along with his colleague, geophysicist Jim Kauahikaua, Clague has crisscrossed Hualalai mountain countless times trying to piece together the volcanic history of Kaʻūpūlehu. The flow originated from a fissure slightly north of a spatter cone named Hinakapoʻula that emitted a jagged, unpredictable stream of lava some 6,000 feet down the mountain. It ran north toward Kīholo, crossed over into Puʻuwaʻawaʻa, and branched off west toward the village of Kaʻūpūlehu at Kahuwai Bay. But there are cultural clues that puzzle the geologists. While awaiting the results of carbon dating, they remain cautious about conclusions.

"Across the Kaʻūpūlehu flow are two wonderful trails," explains Clague. "By 1800, Hawaiian society may have been in a state of transition. We found it hard to believe that such magnificent trails would have been constructed in the 1800s, but they might have in the late 1700s." He and Kauahikaua are searching for clues that would explain why such stellar trails would exist on the Kaʻūpūlehu flow and not on the Huʻehuʻe flow. One trail goes from Kailua to a point just above Puhiapele, according to Kauahikaua, "then makes a beeline down to Kīholo Bay." The second trail starts near the large hill called Puʻuwaʻawaʻa and continues up to the 3,000–4,000 foot level, where, muses Clague, "they probably collected feathers."

"While the Kaʻūpūlehu flow has these wonderful, sophisticated trails—about three feet wide, paved, with curbs—the Huʻehuʻe flow has no such trails across it," he says. Adds Kauahikaua, "It could be that the former is mostly *ʻaʻā* and the latter is mostly *pāhoehoe*, or it could be that Kaʻūpūlehu is somewhat older and the trails were built at a time when Hawaiian civilization was at full strength. I also know that good trails with curbs were built later into the 1830s and 1860s, so we are only speculating about the

*Altered at one end by the Kaʻūpūlehu flow from Huaialai in the late 1700s and at the other end by the 1859 Mauna Loa eruption, Kīholo Bay reigns as one of North Kona's coastal marvels. The Mauna Loa eruption reduced Kīholo's six hundred acres of ponds to three acres and changed its entire ecosystem.*

*This stone wall is all that remains of what was at one time a meeting house and church in Kīholo. The structure was built after 1859, when the village's wooden church was razed and moved in anticipation of the oncoming Mauna Loa flow.*

meaning of these trails and their purposes."

Archaeologist Laura Carter Schuster, who has surveyed the Kaʻūpūlehu *ma kai* area extensively, describes a third trail in the area, a north-south trail marked with an *ahu* (heap of stones) at its south end as one crosses from the Kaʻūpūlehu *ahupuaʻa* to the *ahupuaʻa* of Puʻuwaʻawaʻa to the north. With her findings on this third trail in Kaʻūpūlehu, Schuster agrees with the geologists that Kaʻūpūlehu "could have been an earlier, eighteenth-century flow."

Still visible in the landscape is the island of older dryland forest, a *kipuka* named ʻOwē-ʻowē, created by the jag westward. The imprint of the flow is indelibly etched in the black, brown, and green patterns that undulate seaward between patches of tawny grass. Here, as nowhere else, the story of Pele's wrathful appetite is immortalized in the terrain.

When the goddess of fire struck again in 1859, there was no Kamehameha the Great to appease her. Forty years after Kamehameha's death, Mauna Loa's legendary 1859 eruption came in two phases: the earlier *ʻaʻā* phase that flowed 25 miles to the ocean in eight days, and a *pāhoehoe* phase that ensued for several months and formed a new point on the coastline named Laehou. The eruption's most renowned casualty was Kamehameha's favorite fishpond at Kīholo, a marvel of engineering created in 1812 by thousands of people who carried and arranged acres of rocks. The pond was two miles in circumference and surrounded by a wall six feet high and twenty feet wide. "There were several arches in the wall, which were guarded by strong stakes driven into the ground so far apart as to admit the water of the sea; yet sufficiently close to prevent the fish from escaping," wrote William Ellis upon visiting the island in 1824. "It was well stocked with fish, and water-fowl were seen swimming on its surface." After the eruption, the six hundred acres of ponds that existed before 1859 were reduced to three acres, and all that remained was a lagoon and two inland ponds.

"In this year of Kamehameha IV, Kiholo is closed by the lava," wrote J. H. Kaakua in the October 1859 issue of *Ka Hoe Hawaii*, as translated by the late Mary Kawena Pukui. "It is now only a heap of lava rocks," Kaakua continued. "The Protestant church that stood at Kiholo was removed when the lava flow drew near. The people thought that it would be burned down, so they razed it and took the lumber away lest it be destroyed. But when the lava flow came, it went around the site, leaving it untouched. There is a circle of lava rocks surrounding it and the spot where the church stood remains there like a grave. I believe that if the church had not been razed, it would not have been destroyed anyway."

One hundred and thirty-five years later, as the sun pulls a bright orange curtain on the horizon, Joe Makaʻai stands on the shoreline of his ancestors and declares: "I believe what my grandmother told me: This place is going to change."

# Pele's Wrath

Overleaf—*Fiery skies above Puhiapele ("blown out by Pele") recall the 1801 eruption, when lava from this 300-foot-high spatter cone helped reshape the delta north of Keāhole Point.*

*'Ōhelo berries, from a native shrub in the cranberry family, are the upland food that most pleases Pele. The faithful still make offerings of the berries, shown here in the subalpine zone more than 5,000 feet high on Hualalai.*

ALTHOUGH MORTALS are no match for gods and goddesses, Kamehameha came close. In one of Hualalai's most dramatic encounters, the vaunted ruling chief of the Hawaiian archipelago found himself targeted for battle by a jealous, vengeful goddess who could set volcanoes aflame on a whim. Who else but Pele could bring Kamehameha I face-to-face with his hubris, humble him before his people, and bring him, figuratively, to his knees? The moment of reckoning, the battleground of wits and power, was the 1800–1801 Hualalai eruption.

It was in the fourth year of Kamehameha's rule that Hualalai's lava began cascading down the mountain. It ran in fiery rivers from Hu'ehu'e in the uplands to Keāhole Point and Mahai'ula Bay at the seashore. The historian Samuel Kamakau attributed the event to Pele's desire for the breadfruit of Kāmeha'ikana, which was overrun by the flow, and the delectable *aku* and *'ihi* that flourished at the shoreline.

"Kamehameha was in distress over the destruction of his land and the threatened wiping-out of his fish ponds,' Kamakau wrote. "None of the kahunas, orators, or diviners were able to check the fire with all their skill." Under the advice of his seer and with assurances that he would not be killed, Kamehameha appeased the goddess with an offering of pig and a lock of his own hair, bringing an end to the devastation.

Today, almost two centuries later, Pele is still honored in dance, ritual, and ceremony throughout all the Hawaiian Islands. But who is this omnipotent, unpredictable goddess? In his book, *The Legends and Myths of Hawaii*, King David Kalākaua describes Pele as "the deity most feared and respected, especially on the island of Hawaii." According to him, Pele came to Hawai'i about A.D. 1175,

Ka poʻe kahiko—*the people of old—revered the fire goddess Pele in a time*, wrote historian Samuel Kamakau, *"when the fires had ears and would listen to the words of men." Kamehameha I, depicted in this painting by Herb Kawainui Kane, makes an offering of his hair to Pele during the Hualalai eruption of 1801. The flow stopped, demonstrating Pele's acceptance.* Herb Kane, National Geographic Image Collection.

*The fires of Puhiapele may be quiet for now, but the stones are listening still. Glowing with the light of the sun, Puhiapele's zenith is a prominent presence on Hualalai, an active, not dormant, volcano.*

most likely from Samoa. She had five brothers and eight sisters, who were charged with "the duties of creating explosions, thunders and rains of fire, moving and keeping the clouds in place, breaking canoes, fighting with spears of flame, hurling red-hot masses of lava, and doing whatever else the goddess commanded." The Pele family was "neither connected with, nor controlled by, the supreme gods of Hawaiian worship," and was unknown in Hawai'i prior to the twelfth century, Kalākaua wrote. They arrived as simple human beings "and as human beings lived and died...and superstition subsequently elevated their mortal deeds to the realms of supernatural achievement." Other versions, such as that forwarded by W. D. Westervelt in *Myths and Legends of Hawaii*, put Pele and her family in the realm of the supernatural before their arrival in Hawai'i. With a brother who was a god of sharks and a beautiful sister, Hi'iakaikapoliopele (Hi'iaka-i-ka-poli-o-Pele), who was hatched from an egg warmed in Pele's skirt, Westervelt described Pele and her entourage as possessing powers beyond the mortal.[1]

Pele's legacy is visible today in the charred landscape that is Kekaha, where her supernatural deeds figure prominently in the region's many legends. In keeping with Hawaiian mythology, these legends carry *kaona*, or hidden meaning. They reveal the resourcefulness and ingenuity of a people. They exalt *pono*—moral correctness—and punish the unworthy. Passed down through generations, the legends carry timeless values and imbue the landscape with meaning and power. Even now, the statuesque hill called Kā'ili, prominently visible between Makalawena and Kūki'o, evokes reverence among *kama'āina* like Hannah Springer, who suggests that the *puʻu* appears as an altar in the heartland of Kekaha, especially when approached from the sea or air. Kūʻili, according to *Place Names of Hawaii*, means "memorized temple prayer," and there is a legend attached to it, as there is to many of the fishponds, hills, rocks, and caves sprinkled throughout Kekaha. Through the eruptions, earthquakes, tsunamis, and epochal changes that have left their mark and vanished, Kekaha's mythic legacy remains very much alive.

The chief storytellers of the region were J. W. Isaac Kihe, a school teacher and resident of Puʻuanahulu, and his contemporary, Eliza Maguire, whose book, *Kona Legends*, captures the singular charm of what she called the "tales of 'Plain Every Day Folks'." The wife of John Avery Maguire, Springer's great-great grandfather and the man who founded Huʻehuʻe Ranch in 1886, Maguire gathered and translated the writings of Kihe, who worked for a Hawaiian weekly newspaper in the early 1900s. From Kihe and Maguire we learn one of the several interpretations of the name Kaʻūpūlehu and of many other names and places of Kekaha.

*Kona Legends* recounts the story of an old woman who walked down from the uplands to make a humble appeal to the overseer of the fabled fishpond of Pāʻaiea just as the canoes returned with their bulging catches of *aku*. Walking slowly, leaning on a cane and wearing a *lei* of *koʻokoʻolau* (a medicinal plant that grows in the mountains), she asked for a morsel of fish. She was refused, and when she asked for *palu*—fish head and intestines—she was refused again. The fish were reserved for the chief, the unyielding overseer declared. Returning to the uplands "without even a grain of salt," the woman came upon the home of a man named Kupulau, who invited her to dinner and then gave her a fish to take with her on her journey home.

The old woman, who was actually Pele in disguise, instructed her host to place *lepa*—banners of white *kapa*—at the back of the house and on the fence, telling him, "there will be a night of great doings, and tonight may be the night, and you will have your *ununu* (protection) ready against any evil befalling you."

That night, Pele made her way to Manu-ahi, a quiet village in the uplands of Huʻe-huʻe, near Puhiapele, where she found two sisters roasting *ʻulu*, or breadfruit. The sister named Kolomuʻo told Pele she roasted the *ʻulu* for the goddess Laʻi, while the other sister, Pāhinahina, said her *ʻulu* was for the goddess Pele. Unaware that the stranger before her was Pele, Pāhinahina generously shared her *ʻulu* with her. After learning that the two girls lived in the same house, Pele advised Pāhinahina to tell her parents to place a *lepa* on her side of the house, to mark the boundary between the dwellings of the two sisters.

That was the night of the Hualalai eruption, when lava destroyed the breadfruit grove at Kāmehaʻikana and filled the fabled Pāʻaiea fishponds at the seashore. From Kawahaopele (Ka-waha-o-Pele, the mouth of Pele) in the uplands, the fiery lava flared, dwindled, and erupted again at Kaiwiopele (Ka-iwi-o-Pele, the bone of Pele), and continued on its downward course. Near a hill called ʻAkahipuʻu—today the family graveyard of Springer's ancestors—the lava stream grew until it covered the southern end of the

*Overleaf—The double-lobed Kūʻili ("memorized temple prayer") rises in the distant left like an altar in the heartland of Kekaha.*

*The stories of Kekaha are immortalized in the writings of J. W. Isaac Kihe, left, writer and champion of the Hawaiians at the turn of the century, pictured here with his wife, Kaimu Kihe, Mrs. Joseph Kealalio, and a child, name unknown. Photograph by Louis Sullivan. Courtesy of Bishop Museum Archives.*

house where the sister Kolomuʻo lived. Wrote Eliza Maguire: "The cinder hill of Puhi-A-Pele (Pele's Bon-Fire), which looms like a huge castle of ebony, showing in strong relief against the silvery kukui grove above it, represents the home of one of the two girls roasting bread-fruit which Pele destroyed." Thus was the unkind sister punished and Pāhina-hina spared. Added Maguire, "That is the way the Goddess Pele avenged herself on those who did not acknowledge her as Supreme, and refused to grant her slightest wish."

Joe Makaʻai, to whom this legend is as familiar as a childhood friend, notes that the Puhiapele flow resembles the body of Pele lying down with her head to the north. "If you went there, you could see all the green *kukui* trees and two coconut trees," he says. "The coconut trees represent the older sister and the younger sister." Those two trees remained a landmark until a few decades ago, when they succumbed to drought and fire, he says.

Another version of the breadfruit tale is the one Robert Keakealani handed down to his daughter, Leinaʻala Lightner. According to Lightner, the older sister in the breadfruit legend lived *ma uka*, by Puhiapele, while the younger sister lived with her grandmother at Manuahi, which in Lightner's version of the story is not in the mountains but at the seashore, at Kaʻūpūlehu where the Kona Village Resort is located today. "Pele asked the older sister up *ma uka* for some ʻulu and was refused, but the younger sister at the seaside, who had been taught by her grandparents to respect others, shared her breadfruit willingly," says Lightner. That night, when Hualalai erupted, lava covered the older sister's home in the uplands but spared the younger sister's home at the seaside, which Pele had instructed her to mark with the *lepa*. Because ʻulu means breadfruit and *pūlehu* means to broil or roast, Lightner, like her father before her, believes Kaʻūpūlehu is actually an abbreviation of the name Kaʻūlupūlehu—the roasted breadfruit—referring to the two sisters roasting the ʻulu.

"My father's version was always Kaʻūlu-pūlehu," says Lightner. "That was what he was taught. And he always emphasized the values in this story. When the young girl came home to her grandmother with the four sticks Pele had given her to post the *lepa*, the grandmother told her, 'Don't question, just do what you were told'. That is a value that was taught, as was sharing."

Lightner's version of the story does not go unchallenged, however. Billy Paris, whose grand-aunt was Eliza Maguire, points to evidence in the Kekaha landscape that supports the original version of the legend. Specifically, he says, the shoreline changes wrought by the Hualalai flow from Puhiapele, with which the legend is associated, are seen from just north of Keāhole Point to Mahaiʻula Bay, which is more than three-and-a-half miles south of Kaʻūpūlehu. Moveover, he contends, the village of Manuahi, where the two girls were found roasting breadfruit, was in the uplands rather than on the seacoast. Although many define the word Manuahi as "gratis," or "given freely," the older definition is "firebird," interpreted by some *kamaʻāina* as a reference to the fiery, volcanic history of the land. Says Paris: "The story goes that when Pele caused the eruption, it covered the part of the house where the sassy sister lived, the one who wouldn't give her any breadfruit, and left the part where the good sister

*So important was ʻulu to the regional economy that the breadfruit grove of Kāmehaʻikana, in the uplands of Huʻehuʻe, was one of Pele's two targets in her campaign to humble Kamehameha in the 1800–1801 Hualalai eruption.*

and the parents lived." Paris notes that the rock foundation of the house is still there, on the south side of Puhiapele.[2]

Paris also questions Lightner's assumption that the name Kaʻūpūlehu is an abbreviation of Kaʻūlupūlehu. He cites a different explanation that his grand-aunt, Eliza Maguire, passed down in their family: that Kaʻūpūlehu is an abbreviation of Kaʻimupūlehu. He recounts a legend that explains why: At a time of great famine, a renowned chiefess of Kaʻūpūlehu appealed to her god Kāne for help. In answer to her plea, Kāne placed himself in an *imu* and told her people not to uncover him until they saw the steam—the *puhi*—rising out of the bay. (Some accounts say the chiefess, Kumukea Kalani, was the sister of the god Kāne, and that is why the surf of Kaʻūpūlehu is named Kumukea.) When the *puhi* appeared in the water offshore, the people uncovered the *imu*. According to Paris, it was overflowing with breadfruit, taro, and other food, and the famine was broken by a bountiful feast. "So we go by the name Kaʻimupūlehu-a-ke-akua," he says. The name means "the imu in which the god was baked."[3]

Yet another version of the story[4] has Kāne disguised as a young man who married the daughter of the chief of Kaʻūpūlehu. The young man gained a reputation as a slothful, worthless husband who slept incessantly and never worked. Through his wife, however, he mobilized the villagers to gather wood and build an *imu*, in which he was buried along with taro and a *lehua* tree from the mountains. Later, he reappeared at the ocean, emerging out of the spring. Only after the feast was unearthed from the *imu* did he

*This anchialine pond in Kaʻūpūlehu is part of the basal spring system near where Kāne is purported to have emerged from the shoreline spring known as Waiokāne.*

*Kaʻūpūlehu contains one of the island's two largest brackish springs, discharging, according to* Geology and Ground-Water Resources of the Island of Hawaii, *up to fifty gallons per minute during low tide. The springs of Kaʻūpūlehu, including this one on the grounds of the Kona Village, were a rare and precious resource that allowed permanent habitation along an otherwise parched coastline. With their lips or gourds, the Hawaiians skimmed the surface where the fresh water floated.*

reveal his true identity as the god Kāne.

The spot where the *puhi* rose out of the ocean is known today as Waiokāne (Wai-o-Kāne, the waters of Kāne), and is marked by a freshwater spring that bubbles out of the rocky reef at low tide, and at high tide percolates into the ocean, creating a visible, tangible, vibrating column of fresh water. Even now, those who know the spring ascribe to it a certain salutary transcendence, a sacredness. Instead of carrying empty gourds, modern-day drinkers brace themselves with their hands on the surrounding reef, lower their lips to the spring, and drink—underwater. One account[5] holds that menstruating women may not approach the spring, and anyone who dives into it twenty-five times, in intervals of five, in the morning and in the evening, will achieve miraculous healing. "The *'uhane* (spirit) here is very much alive," notes Lightner.

The legend of Kāne is a pivotal story of the region, and the spring, also called Waikāwili (mixed water), is its most enduring physical landmark. But because Kekaha was essentially dry and arid, the people who lived there required other sources of water. Neighboring Kūki'o Beach, also known for its bubbling springs of sweet, fresh water, was a welcome resource for the local *kama'āina*, its basal springs fattened when rains in the uplands percolated seaward through subterranean layers. Moisture was also captured in caves and underground tubes such as Mākālei, located in the uplands of Hu'ehu'e and immortalized in a lengthy, thirteenth-century Hawaiian legend recorded by Isaac Kihe. According to Kihe scholar Kepā Maly, the story of Mākālei ran as a serial for eight months in 1928 in *Ka Hoku O Hawaii*, a Hawaiian language weekly. Kihe wrote at the turn of the century through the early twentieth century, recounting Hawaiian legends with the intimate knowledge derived from a vital connection to his *kūpuna* and their past. Kihe's legends, wrote Maly, "are a bridge, an opportunity for us to catch a glimpse of how the people lived upon the land," and that included the gathering of water.

"The Cave of Makalei," translated by Maly and appearing in abbreviated form in *Kona Legends*, tells the story of a family that moves from Oʻahu to Kekaha and, despite a debilitating shortage of water, achieves extraordinary success in farming. In tracing the family's movements up and down the *ahupuaʻa* in search of water, arable land, and fish, the story is a remarkable parable about *pono*, resourcefulness and ingenuity.

Mākālei was the youngest child of Koʻa-mokumoku-o-Heʻeia (Koʻa), a skilled fisherman and farmer, and his wife, Ka-ua-pō'ai-hala-o-Kahaluʻu. After arriving at Kaʻūpūlehu, the father surveyed the dry, barren landscape and asked how the people of the uplands obtained water. Kihe (translated by Maly) wrote: "And Keʻawalena told him that the water came only from the rains. When it rained the waterways (dry rivers), the small and large water gourds, the stone catchments made by placing stones together, are all filled with water. The *pao wai*, or dugout pits, are filled with water and these are the places where water is stored. Additionally, some people have *kaulana wai* (places where water rests) or *ana wai* (water caves) which they use when there is no other water. The water in the caves is *kulu wai*, 'water that drips from the rocks'. Channels of banana stalks are set in place to direct the water into troughs of *ʻōhiʻa* and *wiliwili* wood."

The family settled in the uplands, where Koʻa built water gourds, bowls, and catchments that filled with rain and yielded rich harvests of taro, sweet potatoes, sugar cane, bananas, and *ʻawa*. One day while young Mākālei was out behind the family house near ʻAkahipuʻu, a cold wind rose from the ground and directed his attention to a dark hole. Mākālei called for his father, who lifted some stones surrounding the hole and exposed a water cave. To protect their discovery, Koʻa disguised the entrance as a rubbish heap, and the cave remained a secret known only to father and son. They named it Ke Ana Wai o Mākālei (the cave of Mākālei), or, in Maguire's version, He Ano O Mākālei—"consecrated to Mākālei."

The cave dripped water from its roof and down its sides and was large enough for Koʻa to stand upright in. Working secretly at night, he took logs of *wiliwili* and *ʻōhiʻa* and hollowed them out into vessels for catching, carrying, and storing water. Eventually canoes and troughs filled the interior of the cave and collected enough water to sustain his family through the lengthy dry season.

Koʻa passed his knowledge and skills on to his son Mākālei, who grew into an impeccable young man renowned for his success in fishing and farming. Eventually, however, Mākālei departed Kekaha for the island of Kauaʻi. Years later, on a return visit to Kekaha, he competed in an athletic contest at Kaʻūpūlehu. After winning several events, he asked for water. When Mākālei was told that water was available only in the springs at the shoreline, he disagreed. Finally, he and the area landlord made a wager: If Mākālei could find water, the landlord would have to give him his beautiful daughter in marriage. If not, Mākālei would be beaten to death. Mākālei then made his way to the rubbish heap that concealed the cave, revealed it to all of Kekaha, and returned to Kaua'i with his new wife.

In the unabridged version of the story that appeared in *Ka Hoku O Hawaii*, it is Mākālei's son, Kalei, who returned to Ka'ūpūlehu from Kaua'i and uncovered his father's hidden water cave. Arriving in Kekaha, Kalei learned that his grandfather, Ko'a, had died, and that a shortage of water had made life difficult for his grandmother and relatives. As instructed by Mākālei, Kalei revealed the location of the cave to her, and to all of Kekaha.

It was in such fashion that the legends of Ka'ūpūlehu carried lessons and moral values that retained their appropriateness for generations. But these stories also served other functions, including providing the Hawaiian people with a rich source of entertainment. In the legend of 'Akahipu'u, for example, a group of *menehune*—mythical small people who accomplished prodigious works at night—attempt to steal the peak of an upland hill called 'Akahipu'u and attach it to the top of a hill near the coast named Kū'ili. Maguire, who included the story in *Kona Legends*, lived at Hu'ehu'e, where 'Akahipu'u is located. "The hill of Kū'ili has a depression on its top, and the Menehune thought it would be a fine thing to take the pointed top off 'Akahipu'u and place it in the hollow top of Kū'ili, for a cap," she wrote. The *menehune* pranksters grabbed their sticks of sturdy *kauila* wood and dug and dug, to dislodge the hill, but were thwarted by the crowing of a persistent rooster who, they later discovered, had been appointed by the god Kāne to protect 'Akahipu'u.[6] After the *menehune* had departed, wrote Maguire, "Kaleikini, a person of power and renown, a distinguished warrior, came and with a kauila rod, thrust it nine feet deep, and fastened the hill down firm so that the Menehune could not come again and take it away."

Kekaha folklore contains mischief and humor, as well as ghosts of a more sobering nature—just ask Joe Maka'ai. Maka'ai speaks calmly of his encounter with the night marchers—the restless spirits of departed warriors—who walked with some regularity on the Ka'ūpūlehu shoreline. "I used to walk to Waiakauhi Pond[7] all the time with my grandfather," he recalls. "We would go there to catch *'ōpae* for *'ōpelu*. On our way back one night, a wind blew in from the ocean. Strong wind, but when you came close to shore, it was calm. My grandfather said, 'Come here, your grandma's calling you'. Then he grabbed me and laid me down."

With his head on the ground, his eyes shut tight, and his heart pounding, the twelve-year-old Maka'ai heard voices—many of them. "My grandfather told me, 'Keep looking down, don't look up, and when you hear somebody say 'Alia', that means you have a relative among them'." Maka'ai recalls hearing the chilling sounds of footsteps approaching in the night. "And I heard one voice say, 'Alia'. The word means halt. Then they all stopped and walked away. My grandfather said, 'See, you have family in that crowd. If not, they were going to kill you and me'. I heard it," Maka'ai says. "Loud and clear."

Maka'ai recalls another youthful encounter,

*The shoreline stones of Manini-'ōwali tell a story of unrequited love. Legend holds that Manini-'ōwali, spurned by her betrothed, was turned into stone at the water's edge, while the man she loved, Uluweuweu, and the princess he loved, Kahawaliwali, met similar fates at nearby Kūki'o.*

this one with his family's *'aumakua,* or ancestral spirit. "When I was young, I was told my *'aumakua* was the shark," he says. "I asked my grandmother how I could be related to the shark. She told me that my uncle, who was first-born, died at birth and was buried in the ocean. That's how he became a shark, that's what they told me.

"I was brought up in the Mormon faith, my grandmother was Mormon, too, and my grandfather was strong in the old Hawaiian way. I told my grandmother, 'I don't believe that'. And she said she didn't believe it either." That challenged his grandfather, who urged Maka'ai to accompany him in the canoe one day "so you can see your uncle."

"So I went with him that morning," Maka'ai recalls. "My grandfather and I had paddled about two-and-a-half miles out when I saw this flat piece of land floating in the water. We paddled up to it and my grandfather said, 'Jump on'. He knew that was my uncle. So I hopped on and started cleaning that thing. Then I saw that it had gray and white spots. It was a shark. I jumped right back into the canoe and grabbed the paddle. The shark circled the canoe four times," says Maka'ai. Then it dived underwater and immediately surfaced in front of him, moving its dorsal fin back and forth.

"My grandfather said, 'Say good-bye, he's saying good-bye'. I said, 'I don't believe that'. But the shark stayed there, shaking his fin like that. When I made like that"—Maka'ai waves his hand—"the shark dived. And that was the last time I saw him."

In recounting the story, Maka'ai is unable to conceal his own disbelief, his reluctance to accept what he remembers as experience, as accepted family history. Indeed, in many of the traditional accounts and personal stories of old Hawai'i, the legends and figures loom larger than life, and the lines between myth and metaphor are blurred beyond recognition.

One exception is the legend of Manini'ōwali, which concerns a young woman whose name is now literally etched in stone. Residents of Kekaha know Manini'ōwali as both an *ahupua'a* and a stunning white-sand beach at Kua Bay, immediately to the north of the *pu'u* called Kū'ili and south of Kahuwai Bay.[8] As told by Eliza Maguire, Manini'ōwali is a tale of unrequited love. A boy named Uluweuweu, born in Kūki'o, is betrothed at birth to the girl Manini'ōwali, born on the same day at Manini'ōwali Bay. As the announcement of betrothal nears, Uluweuweu becomes ill, but recovers quickly when the engagement festivities are put off. A *kahuna* is called in and determines that Uluweuweu is lovesick—in love with another woman, the princess Kahawaliwali, beautiful daughter of Po'opo'omino and Kaelea-wa'a, high chiefs in the region. To put an end to the scandal, it is decided that all three—Uluweuweu, Kahawaliwali, and the spurned Manini'ōwali—should be put to death, and the *kahuna* has them turned to stone. According to Maguire, at the edge of the sea at Kūki'o, the stone representing Uluweuweu has "his lower limbs firm and fast, and where the upper part is joined to the firm rock in the ground, is a groove like a door hinge which rocks back and forth when the waves dash against it." (Uluweuweu is also the name of the bay at the Kūki'o land division south of Kahuwai Bay, and Po'opo'omino is a *pu'u* nearby.)

The princess Kahawaliwali, meanwhile,

became a thirty-foot-high stone that juts from the sea at Kūkiʻo, its lower part in two sections said to represent her legs, through which the sea flows continuously. And, because she ran and lay down on the sand before being turned into stone, Maniniʻōwali was imbedded at the ocean's edge at nearby Maniniʻōwali. There, with the ebb and flow of the tide, her form is covered up by the sand or revealed clearly on the beach. On certain nights a string of *manini* (reef surgeonfish) can be seen trailing across the bay like a long necklace, a reminder that the girl's name, Maniniʻōwali, means "string of *manini*."

Maniniʻōwali is part of a Kekaha coastline famous for its beautiful bays and beaches, its freshwater springs, its salt flats and fishponds. Throughout Kaʻūpūlehu, and further south of Maniniʻōwali, at Kaloko Pond in the *ahupuaʻa* of Kaloko, it is also famous for its burial caves. According to historian Samuel Kamakau, Kaloko is the site of the burial cave of Kamehameha I. Although that claim is commonly disputed—and the burial places of *aliʻi* are closely held secrets—Kamakau wrote that the cave, known as an *ana huna*, opens into the side of the pond. This is "where Kameʻeiamoku and Hoapili hid the bones of Kamehameha I so that they would never be found," he wrote. Kamakau also listed Kaloko as the place where Kahekili, the ruler of Maui, his sister, Kalola, and her daughter, the grandmother of Kamehameha III, were buried.

Kaloko is a place of great historical significance. But it is at Luahinewai, at the southern end of Kīholo Bay in the *ahupuaʻa* of Puʻuwaʻawaʻa, that one of the most heroic and chilling acts in all of Hawaiian mythology occurred. Kīholo is a two-mile-wide bay bordered by Luahinewai to the south and Waināliʻi at the north. Luahinewai, a crystalline anchialine pond twelve feet deep in its middle, is purported to be the spot where Keōua, Kamehameha I's rival, stopped on his way to the dedication of Puʻukoholā Heiau in Kawaihae. According to popular legend, Keōua sensed that he would be sacrificed to Kamehameha's war god at Puʻukoholā, thereby sealing Kamehameha's fate as the unifier of the Hawaiian Islands. To ensure that his sacrifice would be imperfect, Keōua stopped at Luahinewai in 1791, bathed himself in its cool, pristine waters, and made an incision on his penis. He then paddled up the coastline to his imminent demise.

The actual historical significance of this magnificent pond has been debated by some who question whether Luahinewai as it exists today is as it was in 1791, when Keōua selected it as the site for his ritual. Changes wrought by geology and volcanic eruptions, such as the Kaʻūpūlehu lava flow, might have altered Luahinewai. The answer to that question lies in the results of carbon-dating analysis, which geologists presently await.

In Hawaiian mythology, it is often difficult to separate history from sentiment and what is objectified from what is created in the body of myth. But as Hannah Springer notes, exaggeration helps us to remember—or, as she more eloquently puts it, "Hyperbole assures us that names will be recalled across vast stretches of time."

*Luahinewai, described by John Papa Ii as the "strange water in the lava...the water with the pretty pebbles," is believed to have been a favored bathing pool of the chiefs. It is also said that a secret cave containing chiefly burials opens into the pool.*

# Blood & Bureaucracy

Overleaf—*High on the hills of Kawaihae, where Maui spies landed in the sixteenth century, Puʻukoholā heiau is the last major religious structure built in Hawaiʻi. It was dedicated with the sacrifice of a major rival of Kamehameha in the late eighteenth century.*

*Petroglyphs like these, in Kaʻūpūlehu, are among the stone records of the people who visited and lived along the North Kona coastline.*

KAMALĀLĀWALU, the feisty ruler of Maui, was bored. In the words of historian Samuel Kamakau, he had grown "weary of continued peace" between his island and the island of Hawaiʻi. It was the late sixteenth century, and the gleam in Kamalālāwalu's eye was about to irrevocably change the course of Hawaiian history. He set his sights on the chiefs of Kohala, Kaʻū, and Kona, three districts of Hawaiʻi island, sparing the chiefs of Hilo because they were related to the chiefs of Maui.

His first plan was espionage. The Maui ruler sent his half-brother and another renowned runner of his region to the west coast of Hawaiʻi island. Their task was to encircle the island as spies and gauge the size of the population, furnishing Kamalālāwalu with an assessment of his adversary's might. The shrewd Maui chief planned to fight only if Hawaiʻi's population was small.

After landing at Kawaihae Bay, twenty-eight miles north of what is today the site of the Keāhole Airport, the chief's half-brother ran south along the coastline trail, among teeming fishponds and vast expanses of blistering lava fields. In one day, the legend goes, he ran from South Kohala through North Kona and into South Kona, and back north to Kawaihae—a distance of nearly a hundred miles. The story is recounted in historian Samuel Kamakau's *Ruling Chiefs of Hawaii* in the entertaining, heroic, hyperbolic fashion of a mythic tale.

According to Kamakau, the half-brother, upon his return, said to his incredulous attendants and hosts: "I went visiting from here to the lava bed and the pond that lies along the length of the land…. I went on the long stretch of sand, to the small bay with a point on that side and one on this side. There are large inland ponds…. I went on to the large

rocky cape below, where there was a small bay with big groves of coconut trees. The land from there on is good, and a small village is located there." Thus he described many of the region's well-known landmarks, including the Kanikū lava bed, the Kīholo fishpond, and the sandy bays and inlets of the Kekaha coastline, clear down to the walled-in ponds of Kaloko and far beyond. From the runner's description of the "sharp ridge like the comb of a cock" and the small cave mouth leading to "smooth, waterworn stones," his attendants determined he had gone nearly fifty miles south before returning. Contemplating the feat, they gushed: "Your swiftness is like that of a god."

The half-brother and his fellow spies circled the island, reporting back to the Maui chief that "there were many houses, but few men" on the island of Hawai'i. Deciding the time was right for an attack, Kamalālāwalu gathered his warriors and counselors and sailed from Maui to Hawai'i, where he landed in Kohala and destroyed throngs before heading for Waimea in the uplands. It was there, while looking seaward, that he realized his spies had erred. Hawai'i island warriors were approaching—in numbers so vast they darkened the hillside like a shadow. "The lava bed of Kaniku and all the land up to Hu'ehu'e was covered with the men of Kona," wrote Kamakau. They blanketed the surrounding lava beds, descended from the mountain called Mauna Kea, and stood waiting in Waimea, covering the plains "like locusts," Kamakau added. Taken by surprise, the Maui forces were expunged in a hail of long and short spears, waterworn stones, and lava rocks. Kamalālāwalu, it is said, died fearlessly.

Kamalālāwalu was not the only chief who coveted the lands of Hawai'i island and recognized the value of its northwest region. These lands—the *kaha* lands—were chiefly lands, scrutinized, inhabited, desired, and fought over for centuries by *ali'i* who valued their benign weather, upland forests and bird-hunting resources, and their bountiful offshore fishing grounds.

Even after the arrival of Captain James Cook in 1778 and the onset of Western contact, the fighting continued—albeit in a different form. Into the archipelago poured firearms, cattle, Christianity, whalers, traders, currency, and a new foreign system of land tenure that culminated in the *Māhele* of 1848. In Kekaha, battles over land that were once fought with spears were decided by cannons and then later, with the advent of the *Māhele*, contested through the courts and a new legalized bureaucracy. Thus endured the long history of desire and conflict that had always characterized these lands.

Among the chiefs of old, Kekaha was a focal point of rivalries for generations. Although many of these rivalries occurred between the rulers of Maui and Hawai'i, they also pitted the various chiefs of Hawai'i island against each other. In the mid-seventeenth century, the *ali'i* of Kona, rulers of the dry, western side of the island, coveted the riches of Hilo, Hāmākua and the 'Ōla'a rainforest near the Kīlauea Volcano, famous for their rare *mamo* and *'ō'ō* feathers, war canoes, and fine tapas (cloth made of pounded bark) that were perfumed and dyed with the rare juices of native ferns. The chiefs of Hilo, on the other hand, were envious of Kona's many treasures. According to Kamakau, they desired

*Coconut trees grace the shoreline of Kīholo, as they did in the sixteenth century. On their journey down the west Hawai'i coastline, Kamalālāwalu's runners from Maui were impressed by Kīholo's massive fishpond and lush coconut grove, and by the ponds of Kaloko, which, some historians claim, contain a secret cave in which the bones of Kamehameha were hidden.*

"warm food and drinking water, and tough and tender fish. Those were the wealth of Kona." In the war that ensued, the chiefs of Hilo prevailed, sealing their victory with a decisive battle at Hu'ehu'e. Afterwards, they slaughtered the defeated Kona chiefs and broke open the region's secret places and burial caves.

The bloody rivalries and struggles between Maui and Hawai'i continued on into the eighteenth century. By that time a new ruler, Kekaulike, had ascended to power on Maui. Much like Kamalālāwalu, his predecessor, Kekaulike was an ambitious chief with a penchant for war and a burning desire to rule Hawai'i island. To realize that end, however, the Maui ruler had to do battle with his brother-in-law, Alapa'i, who had earlier sailed from Maui to Hawai'i and conquered the island's six districts. According to Kamakau, Kekaulike "so delighted in war that he sailed to attack Hawaii. The fighting began with Alapa'i at Kona. Both sides threw all their forces into the fight. Kekaulike cut down all the trees throughout the land of Kona. Obliged to flee by canoe before Alapa'i, he abused the country people of Kekaha. At Kawaihae he cut down all the coconut trees. He slaughtered the country people of Kohala, seized their possessions, and returned to Maui," where he later died of epilepsy.

Kekaulike failed in his attempt to unseat his brother-in-law, and his death did little to end the bloodshed between Maui and Hawai'i. In the mid-1700s, the pendulum of victory swung rigorously and prolonged the

*The Hawaiians were ingenious in their use of the hardy trees of the dryland forest, such as* kauila. *Its dense wood was carved into weapons and implements widely appreciated by warriors, farmers who used the digging stick, fishermen who utilized spears and bats, and women who beat tapa. These implements of* kauila, *the extremely rare* pīkoi lua *(double dagger) and* i'e kuku *(tapa beater), were handed down many generations in the family of Hannah Kihalani Springer.*

*The late 1700s was a time of constant warfare, with Hawai'i's rival chiefs fighting district against district and island against island. Although he was known as the king who unified the islands, Kamehameha was aided in his conquests by a Maui chief named Kahekili, who had consolidated several of the islands, and weakened Kamehameha's rivals, years before his ascent. Displaying the western sartorial influences streaming into Hawai'i, Kamehameha is shown in this 1817 watercolor by an artist, Louis Choris, aboard the Russian ship* Rurick, *one of many carrying European explorers to Hawai'i's shores. Courtesy of Bishop Museum Archives.*

war, favoring first one island, and then the other. In 1754, Kalaniʻōpuʻu ascended to power on the island of Hawaiʻi. During a reign that lasted almost three decades, he too tried, and failed, to conquer Maui. In 1780, two years before his death, he bequeathed his lands on Hawaiʻi to his highest-born son, Kīwalao, and to his son's cousin, Kamehameha. To Kīwalao went the districts of Puna, Kaʻū, and Hilo; to Kamehameha went custody of the war god Kūkāʻilimoku (Kū-kā-ili-moku), and the lands of Kona, Kohala, and Hāmākua.[1]

Kamehameha was the chief who would finally conquer Maui and unite the Hawaiian Islands. Born in the mid-1700s in North Kohala, he came to power in stages. During the 1780s, he won a series of wars with rival chiefs that gave him control of Maui, Molokaʻi, Lānaʻi, and most of Hawaiʻi. In 1791, he solidified his hold on Hawaiʻi by defeating his chief rival and cousin, Keōua, the warrior who sliced his penis in the cold, pristine waters of Luahinewai before being killed and sacrificed at Puʻukoholā. "By the death of Keoua Kuahuula and his placing in the heiau of Puukohola the whole of Hawaii became Kamehameha's," wrote Kamakau. Three years later, in 1794, Kamehameha reconquered Maui, Molokaʻi and Lānaʻi, and the following year he added Oʻahu. Kauaʻi came under his control in 1810.

But it was an occurrence in the waters off Kekaha in 1790, twelve years after British Captain James Cook opened the doors to Western contact (and with it, the shadowy world of cannon, muskets, and metal that Hawaiian chiefs came to covet), that provided Kamehameha with the ammunition he

*Sailing into the waters off Ka'ūpūlehu in 1790, the* Fair American, *in this painting by Herb Kāne, is about to be captured by the chief Kame'eiamoku, who had sworn revenge on the first foreigner he encountered after being struck and humiliated by a trader, Simon Metcalfe. Ironically, the captain who lost his life on the* Fair American *was Thomas Metcalfe, son of the man who struck Kame'eiamoku. Herb Kāne, Kona Village Resort Collection.*

needed to unify the Hawaiian kingdom. The incident, which was one of the great accidents in Hawaiian history, resulted from the actions of Simon Metcalfe, a quick-tempered and high-spirited American fur trader. Metcalfe arrived in the waters off Kekaha after slaughtering more than a hundred natives in Olowalu, Maui. There, local natives had killed one of his sailors and taken a small boat. In a barbarous act of revenge, Metcalfe invited other Hawaiians aboard to trade, then blasted them with the full power of his cannons in what became known as the "Olowalu Massacre."

Metcalfe then set sail for the island of Hawai'i, where he anchored his ship, the *Eleanora*, at Ka'ūpūlehu and proceeded to inflict further indignities: When Kame'eiamoku, the chief of Ka'ūpūlehu, tried to board, Metcalfe struck him with a rope, then fled south down the Kona Coast to Kealakekua Bay.[2] Angered at having been humiliated before his people, the Ka'ūpūlehu chief pledged revenge on the next foreign ship he encountered. In a peculiar twist of fate, that ship was the *Fair American*, a tiny 54-foot schooner captained by Simon's son, Thomas Metcalfe. In the waters off Ka'ūpūlehu, Thomas Metcalfe and all but one of his crew of five met their fate. (The sole survivor, Isaac

*John Young, right, and Isaac Davis, the sole survivor of the* Fair American, *became the two foreigners closest to Kamehameha, who sought their friendship and skills—and western weaponry—for his own military advantage.* Courtesy of Bishop Museum Archives.

Davis, displayed such military pluck that he was spared by the Kaʻūpūlehu chief and went on to become a loyal subject and intimate adviser of Kamehameha.)

The incident was rife with irony, for while the *Fair American* was sailing to its demise at Kaʻūpūlehu, Captain Simon Metcalfe was at Kealakekua Bay searching for his son. When John Young, Metcalfe's boatswain, went ashore at Kealakekua, he was prohibited from returning to the *Eleanora* for fear he would spread the news of the capture of the *Fair American* earlier that day. Kamehameha desired Young as a friend, and also as a foreigner who could instruct him in the use of muskets and firearms. After waiting offshore for several days, Metcalfe finally sailed for the Northwest, where he died not knowing his son's fate.

The *Fair American*, meanwhile, with its four-pound cannon and other instruments of war, became Kamehameha's first foreign vessel in his campaign against the chiefs of Maui, Oʻahu, Kauaʻi, and Molokaʻi. Indeed, emboldened by the military advantage provided by his newly found Western weaponry, Kamehameha went on to unify the Hawaiian kingdom. As Hawaiian historian and artist Herb Kane noted in his book, *Voyagers*, "Without this little schooner, he might well have lost the day, and his life.... And without a chief who could bring the islands under one rule, the subsequent history of these islands would have been radically altered."

Although the *Fair American* incident received a good deal of notoriety, its captor, Kameʻeiamoku, was far more significant in Hawaiian history as a diplomat and war chief, and as a sage and loyal adviser to Kamehameha in his ascent as high chief over the Hawaiian Islands. So great was Kameʻeiamoku's service to the chiefs of Hawaiʻi that he and his twin, Kamanawa, appear on the coat of arms of the Kingdom of Hawaiʻi. Young and Davis, meanwhile, spent their remaining days in Hawaiʻi as confidants and advisers to Kamehameha, who gave them land, wives, attendants, and the rank and privileges of chiefs.

One would like to think that the troubles of the land waned under Kamehameha's rule, but in *Ruling Chiefs of Hawaii*, Kamakau tells us otherwise. "At the taking over of rule by Kamehameha troubles arose," he wrote. "The country as a whole benefited by the uniting of the government under one head, but most of the chiefs and landlords under Kamehameha oppressed the commoners and took away their lands, thus forcing the people who had owned the land to become slaves. 'They put their ears to the fuzz of the treefern', was the saying." Excessive taxation was only one problem. There were greed and oppression in the

*The entourage of Lieutenant Otto von Kotzebue of the Russian imperial navy, one of the many European and American explorers to call upon Hawai'i, is shown visiting Kamehameha in Kailua, Hawai'i island, in 1816. Although received congenially by Kamehameha, Kotzebue was initially regarded with caution because of the hostile attempts of another, unrelated, Russian to take over Kaua'i. Kotzebue's ship,* Rurick, *went on to become the first foreign vessel to exchange salutes at the new fort in Honolulu.* Handcolored lithograph after a drawing by Louis Choris. Courtesy of Bishop Museum Archives.

upper reaches of the hierarchy, prompting Kamakau to add, "These were the hardships endured under the old chiefs down to the time of the reign of Kamehameha III." As lands that were historically coveted—by the chiefs of Hawai'i, their Maui rivals, Kamehameha I and his successors, and their generations of competitors (even the newly arrived *haole*)—Kekaha was especially vulnerable to these pressures.

The self-interest of foreigners compounded the hardships. When Captain George Vancouver introduced cattle to Hawai'i in 1793, he planted the seeds of ranching, an industry that flourished in, and then scarred indelibly, Kekaha's dryland forests and stark savannas throughout the nineteenth century and half of the next. The Hawaiian Islands were becoming an established port for fur, silk, and sandalwood traders, many of them stopping on the western shores of Hawai'i island. The suffering of the commoners increased with trade. The currency of commerce was taking hold in a land-based culture that had fed, clothed, and sustained itself, physically and spiritually, without currency. With the dissolution of the old traditions came Western diseases that significantly reduced the Hawaiian population. The arrival of the first whaling ships in 1819 (the year Kamehameha I died), the toppling of traditional Hawaiian religion after Kamehameha's death, and the arrival of American missionaries in 1820—all these elements profoundly affected and reshaped the Hawaiian culture. Eventually the missionaries won in their arguments that a new system of land tenure—private ownership—would be the saving grace of the Hawaiian race.

But who owned the lands of Kekaha? The early chiefs spilled blood to determine who would rule and feast on the *kaha* lands, and then passed the lands to their heirs in the line of *ali'i* that succeeded Kamehameha I. Among those in control before and during Kamehameha's rule were Kame'eiamoku, the chief of Ka'ūpūlehu at the time of the *Fair American* incident, his twin brother, Kamanawa, and two other "Kona uncles" who were Kamehameha's strongest supporters. Kamehameha bequeathed them the biggest portions of the many lands he had won by conquest. According to Lilikalā Kame'eleihiwa in her book *Native Land and Foreign Desires: Pehea Lā E Pono Ai?*, the Kekaha twins, Kame'eiamoku and Kamanawa, were considered among the most powerful men in the kingdom.

Until the *Māhele* introduced the concept of private land ownership, "ownership of the *'Āina* accrued to whoever was in control of them at the time," Kame'eleihiwa wrote. The *Māhele* also established the Land Commission and gave it the authority to confirm the commoners' requests for land if they paid the required fees. The seeds of bureaucracy were planted, and their greatest victims were the Hawaiian commoners. "Thus, the Land Commission, that body which arose out of foreign suggestion and which was controlled by foreigners, became the new source of *'Āina* in Hawai'i," she continued. "A quiet revolution had been accomplished whereby foreigners now controlled all the *'Āina*...." Ownership of the land, rather than its use—a concept that for Hawaiians was "akin to filing documents for the right to use the air we all breathe"—eventually became the law of the kingdom, said Kame'eleihiwa.

When Kamehemeha died in 1819, his son,

Kamehameha II (Liholiho), succeeded him briefly but significantly—long enough to topple, with Ka'ahumanu (Kamehameha's favorite wife and close adviser), the ancient religion and prohibitions (*kapu*). Ka'ahumanu went on to become the kingdom's most ardent Christian, while Liholiho died at twenty-seven years of age, a mere five years after the death of his father. Liholiho's younger brother, twelve-year-old Kamehameha III (Kauikeaouli), succeeded him for what was to be a thirty-year reign.

Born in Keauhou, Kona, in 1814, Kamehameha III was brought as a child to 'O'oma, in the southern region of Kekaha, and lived there until he was five years old. He forever retained a special fondness for the region. Even before he declared the *Māhele* in 1848, he was closely advised by foreign officials whom he had placed in positions of power, and was highly influenced by the growing demands of Westerners to own land. Native Hawaiians, fearing the oncoming changes, voiced their unrest with a petition dated June 12, 1845, and signed by more than three hundred citizens of Kona.[3] Inscribed in Hawaiian, the petition appealed passionately and prophetically to Kamehameha III: "You chiefs must not sell the lands to the white men nor to the foreigners.... If you wish to sell or lease the lands you should sell or lease them to your own people.... If the chiefs are to open this door of the government as an entrance way for the foreigners to come into Hawaii, then you will see the Hawaiian people going from place to place in this world like flies."

The appeals and unrest failed to deter the king from declaring the *Māhele*, and three years later, the petitioners' worst fears were

*Kamehameha III, top, and Kamehameha V, middle, were among the scions of the Kamehameha dynasty who favored and owned various* ahupua'a *in Kekaha. Kamehameha III is remembered as the king who declared the Māhele in 1848 and thus set the wheels in motion for the new western bureaucracy. Two Kekaha chiefs, Kame'eiamoku and Kamanawa, were esteemed advisers to Kamehameha I who were selected to appear on the Hawaiian Coat of Arms, left.* Courtesy of Bishop Museum Archives.

*Kamehameha V, who so valued Ka'ūpūlehu and Kaloko that he requested these lands for himself at the time of the Māhele, was one of several relatives who bequeathed vast tracts of land to Ruth Ke'elikōlani, right. In turn, Ke'elikōlani left her 'āina to Bernice Pauahi Bishop, left. Pauahi was the largest holder of chiefly lands in the islands and her trust, The Kamehameha Schools/Bishop Estate, today owns 180,000 acres in North and South Kona. Courtesy of Bishop Museum Archives.*

realized. In the first three months of 1848, Kamehameha III and 245 chiefs divided the lands of the archipelago among themselves. The king held nearly 2.5 million acres, or more than sixty percent of the total land, while the chiefs received 1.5 million acres. The king then divided his lands into his personal lands, called Crown Lands, and the lands set apart for government control, called the Government Lands. Although the right of commoners to own land came a year later, in 1849, many of them had no understanding of the application process, and only nine percent of the Hawaiian population received land.

Among the lands Kamehameha III selected for himself were two of Kekaha's *ahupua'a*—Haleohi'u and Pu'uwa'awa'a further north, with its valuable Kīholo fishpond and rich forest resources. In the Kamehameha line of succession, Kamehameha V (Lot Kapuāiwa) inherited thirty-five parcels of land on Hawai'i that included the *ahupua'a* of Ka'ūpūlehu, Kohanaiki, and Kaloko.[4] Kaloko itself consisted of 4,230 acres.[5] Kamehameha V formally requested for himself Ka'ūpūlehu and Kaloko, regions of great wealth in upland and shoreline resources. (Even King David Kalākaua, the "Merrie Monarch" who ruled Hawai'i from 1874 until his death in 1891, leased the *kaha* lands from his kingdom for his own personal enjoyment.)

As far back as the 1700s, Kaloko and Honokōhau in the southern reaches of Kekaha were considered especially valuable because of their extensive fishponds and natural landing areas for canoes, and because of their proximity to Kamehameha's home and *heiau* in Kailua. They were thriving, populated fishing villages. When Kenneth P. Emory and Lloyd J. Soehren prepared their "Archaeological and Historical Survey, Honokohau Area, North Kona, Hawaii" in 1971 for the

*These mounds of stone, near the boundary between Kaloko and Honokōhau, two of the* ahupuaʻa *of Kekaha, are significant, says archaeologist Laura Carter Schuster, because of their proximity to a large anchialine pond associated with ritual bathing. Named Kahinihiniʻula, the chiefs' bathing pool at Kaloko was described in the travels of Ka-Miki, recorded by Isaac Kihe and translated by Hawaiian cultural specialist Kepā Maly.*

Bernice Pauahi Bishop Museum, they found seventy-two archaeological sites along the coastal sections of these *ahupuaʻa*. They included fifty house sites, four *heiau* (pre-Christian stone temples), a *hōlua* (toboggan) slide, fishponds, salt pans, burial sites, and petroglyphs. Kamehameha V's cousin received the lands of Honokōhau 1 with its large fishpond, ʻAimakapaʻa. With its smaller fishpond, ʻAiʻopio, Honokōhau 2 went to the husband of Princess Ruth Keʻelikōlani, a Kamehameha I descendant. This string of heirs comprised the highest *aliʻi* (chiefs or chiefesses) who received lands in the *Māhele*.

When she died in 1883, Ruth Keʻelikōlani, who had inherited lands from her first husband, her father, her half-sister, and her half-brother, Kamehameha V, bequeathed her *ʻāina* to Bernice Pauahi Bishop, who later became the largest owner of the high chiefs' lands in Hawaiʻi.[6] Pauahi Bishop's inherited lands also included the *ahupuaʻa* of Makalawena, inherited from her cousin, the chiefess ʻAkahi. The great-granddaughter of Keōua, the warrior king offered as Kamehameha's sacrifice at Puʻukoholā, ʻAkahi recognized Makalawena's rich wetlands and *ʻōpae*-rich ponds when she claimed those lands in the *Māhele*. These and other lands comprised Pauahi's vast inheritance. Upon her death in 1884, these lands formed the Bernice Pauahi Bishop Estate, a trust benefiting the Kamehameha Schools for Hawaiian children. As Hawaiʻi's largest private landowner, the Bishop Estate remains a major factor in the future of Hawaiʻi island, and of Kekaha in particular. Of the 297,011 acres of land the Estate owned on Hawaiʻi island in 1995, 180,000 acres were in North and South Kona. While the ponds and wetlands and sun-drenched bays of Kekaha provided food and comfort for the ancients, their value accrued materially with time. One cannot help but wonder: Did the Bishop Estate and its predecessor *aliʻi* realize the ultimate value of the *kaha* lands? The new vocabulary—real estate—planted by the *Māhele* ensured that Kekaha's allure would continue, if not burgeon, in modern times.

Throughout the centuries, the residents of North Kona have known the uncertainties of impermanence. Whether displaced by lava, tsunami, drought, or the tide of foreign ways, the natives of Kekaha have adapted and endured. In the late 1800s, facing increasing displacement by the effects of the *Māhele* and the lure of urban life, the stalwart residents of North Kona again united their voices in an appeal to the government, echoing their counterparts in the pre-*Māhele* Kona petitions of 1845 (which, judging by history, had not

*The Kona petitions of the mid-to-late 1800s, several of them in the elegant hand of J. W. Isaac Kihe, express the concern of the Kona residents as they find themselves increasingly landless following the declaration of the Māhele. This document asks that 115 acres of the government lands of North and South Kona be made available as homesteads for the native Hawaiian petitioners, who "are without homes, and are destitute and have no place to live on." The petition, declaring that "the minds of your servants hope and desire to have a place to live on in the future, and to have home for all time," poignantly reflects the displacement of the Hawaiians that began with the Māhele.* Courtesy of Hawaii State Archives.

been addressed). In the impeccable penmanship of J.W.H. Isaac Kihe, a resident of Pu'uanahulu and "Representative of the natives who have no land," several petitions to the Minister of Interior asked that the North Kona government lands be subdivided into homesteads and "given to the native Hawaiians who are destitute and poor...." One petition, dated July 3, 1890, and signed by sixty-four Hawaiians, asked that the lots already subdivided by the government but lying idle be leased to the "poor and needy" for five cents per acre because "they are rocky and pahoehoe lands only left, and the number of acres being about three thousand and over...." The petition also asked that the government lands of Kaulana, Mahai'ula, Kūki'o 1 and 2, Kalaoa 5, and 'O'oma 1 be surveyed and subdivided for natives. In 1893, the Kingdom of Hawai'i was illegally overthrown by American forces and non-native missionary and business interests. Five years later, in 1898, all Government and Crown Lands—1.75 million acres—were ceded to the United States.

Ironically, it was under the regime of the Republic of Hawai'i, formed by those who overthrew the Monarchy, that native Hawaiians were able to claim lands for homesteading under the Land Act of 1895. Whether the homesteading section of the Act was in response to the Kona petitions can only be surmised. However, statistics reveal that the Act was flawed, and that Hawaiians received far fewer lands than Americans. According to a 1969 report of the Legislative Reference Bureau, in the year following the 1895 Land Act, 129 Native Hawaiians obtained 3,873 acres in leases and other purchases allowed by the Land Act, while fifty fewer Americans (seventy-nine) obtained 1,647 acres more than the Hawaiians. A year later, 101 Hawaiians owned nearly 2,630 acres in leases while forty-one fewer Americans held 1,934 acres more.

Larry Kimura, Hawaiian scholar and Hawaiian Studies professor at the University of Hawai'i at Hilo, recalls that his great-grandfather, James N. Purdy, became an early beneficiary of the 1895 Act when he obtained, for a dollar per year, a 999-year homestead lease in Kapalaoa, at the northern boundary of Kekaha. "He had to show that he was homesteading and harvesting, using the land," says Kimura. "The original intent of the Act was to provide for the Hawaiian people so they could make a livelihood of it. My great-grandfather planted *hau, kou, hala,* and *loulu* to improve the property." He also gathered untold pounds of sandstones and coral and carried them, on his back, along the shoreline from Keawaiki to Kapalaoa (a distance of two miles) so he could repair and embellish the stone walls on his homestead. For other improvements required by the homestead lease, lumber was floated in from boats in the bay.

In his 1968 report, *Kapalaoa Homestead Life,* Kimura contrasted the richness of Kapalaoa's life and culture with the harshness of its physical conditions. While residents continued to live off the sea and land, the lack of drinking water, access, and electricity became increasingly acute with time. In 1920, Kimura wrote, a government official responsible for checking on the homesteaders lamented: "It took me 4 hours to get to this place on horseback over the worst trail I have ever had the misfortune to travel.... To give you an idea, it

*At Kūki'o on the shoreline of Kekaha, where generations of Hawaiians both toiled and enjoyed their leisure, the lava features of the* kaha *lands are visible above and below the water. Spring-laden Kūki'o welcomed upland dwellers on their holidays, as well as travelers making the hot, long, north-south journey between Kailua and Kawaihae.*

took me an hour to pass thru a lava (a'a) flow, with its loose linkers; then another hour over pahoehoe then two hours of hard uphill climbing. Not a breeze and not a sound outside of your own breathing and puffing of the horse... The distance is only 10 miles."

Through the efforts of Robert Hind, a legislator and founder of Pu'uwa'awa'a Ranch in 1893, the lands of Pu'uanahulu were also made available for homesteaders, many of whom, at the time, were under his hire. Kimura says his uncle, Joe Maka'ai, one of the last persons alive to have lived at Ka'ūpūlehu, was allowed to remain there as long as he could. "He said, 'This is Bishop Estate land, but this is where we come from'," says Kimura. "He is the last of many generations who had been born and raised there. Everyone knew that these people belonged to the land."

Maka'ai and his cousin, the late Robert Keakealani, are cherished *kūpuna* (elders) because they form a vital link in Kekaha's transition from traditional times to the modern. It was in their vast backyard, with their families and friends, that the beginnings of commerce manifested in the late 1800s as small general stores, ranches, coffee plantations, churches, and schools sprouted up and reinvigorated the stark lands of Kekaha. These activities, services, and resources further connected the many *ahupua'a* of Kekaha. Eventually, however, the effects of depopulation and displacement from the *Māhele*, and the irrevocable turnarounds in what had been a subsistence economy, caused many to migrate to the more commercial areas of Kailua and, further north, Kawaihae.

In some ways, the Kekaha of today is not far removed from the rugged lands coveted by Kamalālāwalu and traversed by his spies in the sixteenth century. Blood has spilled on the lands and the lands have changed hands many times, but the broad horizons of *pāhoehoe* and crumbly *'a'ā* lava still dominate the expansive landscape, as they have from the beginning. These days, however, goats and donkeys roam Kekaha and the undesirable, non-native fountain grass lines the landscape in an ominous layer of tawny velvet. Pele is still feared, though neither seen nor heard. Ranchers have dug in their heels and staked their fortunes in the arid lands of Kekaha, some of them vanishing under the obsolescence of the industry and the weights and demands of the twentieth century. Fishermen come to the shoreline for the day, but they no longer live there. Still, one can easily imagine—almost hear—the footsteps of the past on the ancient trails, where warriors, traders, and hardy residents toiled in the heat on their forays from *ma uka* to *ma kai*. No longer are the hills of Kekaha black with warriors and heavy with the stench of battle. The drama of Kekaha is ever unfolding, but the struggles are bloody no more.

# Astride on the Kaha Lands

*Overleaf—A single paniolo, sometimes two, is all it takes to move Hualalai Ranch's Santa Gertrudis cattle from one pasture to another. In a single day, the cowboys' tasks may take them from 1,900 to 6,000 feet in elevation.*

*Puʻuwaʻawaʻa Ranch paniolo Robert Keakealani, middle, and his brother, David Keakealani, right, separate the cattle before branding them. The photo, taken in the late 1950s in the area of Hualalai called Henehene, shows a stone corral built before Robert Keakealani was born in 1916. Out of the ranch's more than twenty paddocks, only a handful are made of stone.* Courtesy of Leinaʻala Lightner.

WIND has always been the harbinger of change in Kekaha. The people of the region consider the winds the ultimate messengers of the landscape. Like intimate friends, the winds have names and a palpable presence. There is the cold wind from Maui, the *Hoʻolua*, that ripples the waters of Waiakauhi Pond on its way to Kailua, where it becomes the cold wind from Kekaha. There is the *ʻEka*, the prevailing wind of Hualalai, which blows softly from her slopes and calls forth the canoes for good fishing. There is the forceful *Mumuku* that kicks up the surf in the early afternoon, warning the fishermen to stay home. From the mountains swirls the rare and devastating *Kūhonua*, and from Kawaihae there is the sweeping, moving *Nāulu* shower. From the uplands of Waimea comes the *Kaumuku*,[1] and from Maui across the channel, the sudden, warm *Hulumano*, warning of the coming of the night marchers.[2] Moving lightly from ocean to shore, the *ʻŌlauniu* pierces the coconut leaves, making a rustling sound that soothes and heals. When the northeast tradewind, *Aʻe*, cools the baked lands of Kekaha, the *kūpuna* whisper, *"Ola i ke ahe lau makani"*—when a warm day is relieved by a breeze, "There is life in a gentle breath of wind."[3]

The winds were breathing new life into Kekaha at the turn of the nineteenth century. Cattle, horses, and donkeys were bringing greater ease and mobility. For the first time, the hardy people of the region could travel off the ground and without a canoe, carrying their trade items—*poi*, woods, *lau hala*, fish—on beasts that shared their burdens as they navigated the *ma uka—ma kai* and coastal trails in the blistering heat. *Paniolo*—cowboys—and a new life astride accompanied these animals, and with them came ranching, first with Huʻehuʻe Ranch, founded in 1886, and then Puʻuwaʻawaʻa, established in 1893.[4]

By the time the dust had settled from the first cattle and goat drives, commerce—a new value and use for the land—had taken root, forever changing the region and its people. As early as 1880, the lands of Kekaha yielded small cash crops and businesses: general stores, at least three goat ranches, a sheep ranch, a blacksmith, and four small coffee plantations.[5] These efforts to create a cash economy, coupled with the larger-scale cattle ranches of Puʻuwaʻawaʻa and Huʻehuʻe, created dynamic changes in the culture and landscape. New comforts had come to the *kaha* lands, and with them, new challenges and problems.

They came in waves, beginning with British Captain George Vancouver's gift of the first cattle to Kamehameha I in 1793. Eyeing the cattle as a possible new resource for Kamehameha's kingdom, Vancouver suggested a ten-year *kapu*, or taboo, on the slaughter of the animals—an idea that backfired dramatically. As Vancouver had envisioned, the cattle multiplied—so much so that "they became quite a nuisance," wrote Marie D. Strazar in *Nā Paniolo o Hawaiʻi*. "They frequently destroyed upland native forests and occasionally came down from their mountain holdouts to ravage the gardens and taro farms of unsuspecting villagers." Horses, which had arrived ten years after the cattle (also as a gift to Kamehameha), were the key component in efforts to hunt and control the beasts. By the time the first missionaries arrived in 1820, rough-and-tumble bullock hunters were thundering across Kekaha on their horses in hot pursuit of the dangerous wild cattle that roamed the land. Uninitiated in the skills of roping, which were to arrive a decade later with the *paniolo*, the hardy mountain men, most of whom were *haole*, trapped the wild cattle in pits.[6]

The bullocks were just one in a series of well-intentioned gifts from the British that eventually ran amok. After Captain James Cook introduced goats to the Islands in 1778, they, too, became an environmental menace, particularly on Hawaiʻi island. The same was true of sheep, which quickly established themselves on Mauna Kea and Hualalai after being introduced by the British in the 1790s. Granted royal protection like cattle, the sheep became an ecological liability in the upland native forests where they thrived. When efforts to raise sheep as an economic crop failed due to fleece contamination from the barbed, pesky Spanish needle, the demand grew among ships and traders for leather, beef, tallow, and hides. With the commercial value of cattle on the rise, ranching became an industry, and Kekaha its native soil.

"Ranching allowed many of the *kamaʻāina* an opportunity to continue their intimate relationship with the landscape of their elders," muses Hannah Springer, a descendant of the family that founded Huʻehuʻe Ranch. "In some cases, if the ranchers were fair, moral people, they were the new *aliʻi* that replaced the old. Ranching certainly allowed many families a continued relationship with the oceans and forests of their ancestors."

Ranching had its beginnings in Hawaiʻi three or four decades before many of the western states. Years before California, Texas, and the Pacific Northwest became part of the United States, Hawaiians were riding, roping, and breeding cattle on Hawaiʻi island. The Horatio Alger of island ranching was

*Using horses and cattle that were gifts from the British in the late eighteenth and early nineteenth century, the* paniolo *had their beginnings on Hawaiʻi island long before the western states. Although ranching activity in Kekaha has dwindled markedly since its heyday, some paniolo, like Hualalai Ranch manager Franklin Boteilho, still spend much of their time astride.*

John Palmer Parker, a New England sailor. Parker went from sailing to the shipping business and, by 1815, during his second visit to Hawai'i, had become the caretaker of King Kamehameha's royal fishponds. Before long, he made a name as a bullock hunter nonpareil and a *paniolo* of growing renown. He married Hawaiian chiefess Rachel Kipikane, a descendant of Kamehameha I. For a token ten dollars, he bought two acres of land from Kamehameha III, while his wife acquired six-hundred-forty acres by virtue of her royal birth. Thus was born Parker Ranch, situated in the neighboring district of South Kohala. It eventually became the largest ranch under individual ownership in the United States, supporting 50,000 head of cattle on 225,000 acres. It was Parker's descendants who forged the frontiers of ranching in Hawai'i and established the other major ranches of Hawai'i island.

One of those descendants was John Avery Maguire, a man of half-Hawaiian blood, who founded Hu'ehu'e Ranch in 1886. Maguire started Kahuā Ranch in Kohala before turning his attention to Hu'ehu'e on the flanks of Hualalai. Maguire leased the lands of Ka'ūpūlehu from the Bernice Pauahi Bishop Estate and inherited lands belonging to his first wife, Luka Hopula'au (the great-great grandmother of Hannah Springer), after her death in 1898.[7] He augmented these holdings with the lands of Kaloko that he acquired from Queen Kapi'olani. When Maguire died in 1919, the man who married his granddaughter, Arthur J. Stillman, took over management of the vast Hu'ehu'e ranch lands. Expanding through the generations, Hu'ehu'e Ranch went on to become one of the top twenty landholdings in Hawai'i. At its largest, the ranch consisted of 24,000 fee simple acres;

with the leases it obtained from the Bishop Estate, the acreage totaled about 40,000. The ranch lands, some of the finest real estate in Kona, sprawled over the flanks of Hualalai, from the uplands to the shoreline of Kekaha, all the way to Hōlualoa and beyond. The sweeping acreage encompassed the resources and beauty of the white-sand beach at Kūki'o, the fishponds at Kaloko, the pasture lands at Hōlualoa, and the forested lands of Kaloko *ma uka*. "We had coastal resources that most other ranches didn't have," notes Hannah Springer. "Beneath the Hu'ehu'e lands flow rich water resources, making them water-rich lands even if the water wasn't readily available from the surface. The forest of Kaloko was a wonderful cloud forest, rich with *'alalā* (Hawaiian crow) and a tremendous amount of biodiversity."

Legislator Robert Hind and *paniolo* Eben Low founded Kekaha's other major ranch, Pu'uwa'awa'a, in 1893. The *ahupua'a* of Pu'uwa'awa'a forms a large, sweeping coast-to-upland wedge in the northern section of Kekaha, extending fifteen miles from the sea to within a mile of the summit of Hualalai. Its six miles of seacoast encompass Kīholo, the major shipping port for the ranch until the 1930s, and the bay whose large fishpond was eradicated by the 1859 Mauna Loa lava flow. When Hind and Low established Pu'uwa'awa'a Ranch in the upper reaches of the *ahupua'a*, Kīholo at the shoreline bustled with the activities of five families, a church, a school with twenty-one students, four two-story houses, and the streams of cattle, goats, pigs, and turkeys that the cowboys noisily assembled to be shipped.[8] The cattle were made to swim out to rowboats which shuttled them to a waiting steamer, where they were hoisted aboard. To feed the cattle, and for use as fencing, fuel, and shade, the ranchers planted bundles of *kiawe* (mesquite) along the coastline.[9] In the uplands of Pu'uanahulu where most of the ranch hands lived, rich yields of corn, melon, tomatoes, peaches, sweet potatoes, and taro lined the horizon and fed upland and coastal dwellers, as well as people on the neighbor islands. Three to five tons of corn were shipped to O'ahu each year.[10]

Pu'uwa'awa'a Ranch eventually became the second largest in Hawai'i, with 15,000 head of cattle grazing on 40,000 acres. Former ranch manager Billy Paris, born in 1922, has vivid memories of the ranching life as it once existed. He can still recall the wild-and-woolly cattle drives across the vast upper reaches of Hualalai and Mauna Loa. He can

*Pānānā, shown in this photograph from Kukui'ohiwai, was the wife of Sam Parker, cousin of Eben Low of Pu'uwa'awa'a Ranch. Parker, grandson of the founder of Parker Ranch, was also Queen Lili'uokalani's Minister of Foreign Affairs at the time of the overthrow of the Monarchy. Courtesy of Hannah Kihalani Springer.*

The hills of Puʻuanahulu and Puʻuwaʻawaʻa can be seen from the shores of ʻAnaehoʻomalu, which marks the northern boundary of Kekaha. Puʻuwaʻawaʻa, visible in the distant right, was a center of ranching activity at the turn of the century. The two large puʻu form the oldest lava flows on Hualalai, from the Pleistocene period more than one hundred thousand years old. The Puʻuwaʻawaʻa volcanic cone, eight miles from the coast, is the Islands' richest source of trachyte pumice, which contains a sizable amount of obsidian, a volcanic glass the Hawaiians fashioned into cutting tools.

*Robert Keakealani tows a steer to a boat at Kailua Bay in the late 1940s. Only the most skilled cowboys with the strongest horses were selected for this task. "It was an art,"* recalls Leinaʻala Lightner, Keakealani's daughter. *"If the boat man missed the rope, the cow would swim away, and the cowboy and his horse would have to swim further to catch it. If they didn't, the cow would swim to Huliheʻe Palace."* Courtesy of Leinaʻala Lightner.

still taste the homemade butter they made on the ranch, smell the beef that was hung in the open air to cure, and feel the coolness of the butter house and the rarefied heights of the summit areas. It was an honest, straightforward life, he says, as rich in human decency as it was in toughness and bravado. The *paniolo* started their day before sun-up with a breakfast of hot stew and rice to warm themselves in the chill mountain air. Then they went to work on horseback, their days spent taming cattle, mending fences, and repairing water tanks. "We were free riders," says Paris, who recalls that his uncle, Eben Low, one of the founders of Puʻuwaʻawaʻa Ranch, "liked to see us young guys ride like he did. He lost his forearm in his thirties, in a roping accident up on Mauna Kea. He had two artificial attachments for the severed arm: one was a wooden hand with a glove on it, that he used when he was socializing, and the other was a hook that he used for roping and riding." Eben Low, Paris declares proudly, was a "real rough rider."

*Paniolo* like Eben Low were strong, rugged individuals. They could ride a horse all day through dust, wind, rain, and cold. They were keenly attuned to nature and possessed extraordinary skills with animals. Cattle had to be branded and earmarked, and the males castrated. Horses needed to be broken and tamed. Paris remembers that Robert Keakealani and Joe Makaʻai used to track and train wild donkeys. "Robert would pick *kiawe* beans and drop them as feed," he says. "Each day, he'd put the *kiawe* closer and closer to

the fence. Finally, one day, he'd lure the donkey inside the fence, and they'd shut the gate."

The ranching lifestyle brought together a variety of cultures. Hawai'i's *paniolo* learned their skills from the Indian, Spanish, and Mexican *vaqueros* who arrived in Hawai'i in the 1830s at the behest of Kamehameha III. As the years passed, the *paniolo* came to include Hawaiians and part-Hawaiians, Portuguese, Filipinos, Japanese, Caucasians, and all combinations thereof. Hawaiian and part-Hawaiian *paniolo* took readily to the rigors of ranching life, although to hear Paris tell it, there were those who belittled their skills. A former ranch manager once told him, "All you got here is a bunch of dumb *kanakas*," he says. "I resented that comment because I have Hawaiian blood. I tried to help the workers to be more independent. I got their wages raised. I gave them paint to spruce up their houses.

*Robert Keakealani, above, leads a flock of sheep across the Kawaihae Pier in the 1940s. At right, Keakealani is among the cowboys taking a break while towing steer out for shipping at Kailua Bay. The old Akiona Store, which supplied necessities for the* paniolo, *is visible near where a restaurant complex stands today. Courtesy of Leina'ala Lightner.*

Queen Liliʻuokalani, who ruled Hawaiʻi from 1891 to the overthrow of the Hawaiian Monarchy in 1893, was a frequent guest in the kaha lands. Her signature, above left, is the first on this page of the Huʻehuʻe guest book and would be recognized only by her closest friends. Surrounded by Aileen Maguire, the granddaughter of John Avery Maguire, and friends, the queen enjoys an excursion at Huʻehuʻe. Guest book courtesy of Hannah Kihalani Springer; photograph courtesy of Bishop Museum Archives.

I'd have the women up to the ranch to be served a formal tea or dinner. That ranch was $120,000 in the hole when I got there. When I left, they were $30,000 in the black, and I did it with those 'dumb *kanakas*.'"

The ranching life revolved around alternate cycles of hard, gutsy work and gracious social interchange. When the work week was over, the ranching community often came together for festive social occasions. Wearing their best *paniolo* regalia, the men and their families played music, danced the *hula*, and sang Hawaiian songs. Hannah Springer notes that in the late 1800s, Huʻehuʻe Ranch welcomed all manner of visitors in the spirit of hospitality. Guests at the ranch ran the gamut, from Hawaiian royalty to those responsible for the demise of the Kingdom of Hawaiʻi in 1893. "Our family guest book carries the signatures of people ranging from Queen Liliʻuokalani, the last Hawaiian monarch, to Sanford P. Dole, president of the Republic of Hawaiʻi," she says. Other guests included Prince Jonah Kūhiō Kalanianaʻole and the author Jack London and his wife. Even David Kalākaua, who presided over the Kingdom of Hawaiʻi from 1874 until his death in 1891, rode horseback across sections of Kekaha that he leased for his own enjoyment.

The convivial rituals of the ranching lifestyle only grew with the decades. Landscape architect and *kamaʻāina* Scott Seymour remembers his elders "sitting, talking story, and stringing these gorgeous *halapepe leis*." The fragrant *halapepe* is a native dracaena of the dryland forest. The creamy yellowish-white flowers, about an inch-and-a-half long, produce full, showy garlands that perfume

Eva Parker, the tall woman at center above, and her friends and relatives, including Aileen Maguire, exhibit the sartorial formality of the ranching era. Above right, the group is at the sixteenth-century heiau, Ahua'umi, in the saddle between Hualalai and Mauna Loa. Some suggest that the stones were Census markers, others that they were related to the practice of astronomy and the marking of celestial events.

Right, John Maguire and his entourage begin their journey from Hu'ehu'e to the beach, circa 1910. The rifles are for eradicating goats. Courtesy of Hannah Kihalani Springer.

*Every spring, Kekaha residents anticipate the fragrant blossoming of the dryland-forest* halapepe, *a native dracaena depicted in this painting by Pilipo Springer of Kukuiʻohiwai.* Courtesy of Hannah Kihalani Springer.

the air and were the unmistakable signature of North Kona in the 1930s. "Back then, everyone wore beautiful leis and *holokū* and *holomuʻu*," Seymour says. "You'd know the moment you smelled freesia that someone had come from Waimea. When someone would approach with a big *pūʻolo* (bundle) carrying a *halapepe* lei, they'd all sigh and say, 'Ah, that's from up north'."

Seymour recalls that when springtime arrived in Puʻuwaʻawaʻa, his mother, Sadie Seymour, would receive a phone call from her friend, Hannah Hind, the sister of Eben and Eliza Low. "Oh, the *halapepe* is in beautiful bloom! Come out and do something," her friend would implore. "My mother would go and make an arrangement for the piano, and the few extra flowers that fell off would be picked up by the cowboys."

Neighborly visits, camaraderie, and the sharing of resources were a large component of the ranching life. Paris recalls that in the late 1950s when Francis Iʻi Brown had his seaside retreat at Keawaiki and the Hinds of Puʻuwaʻawaʻa had Kīholo, "We'd go up and down the coast and visit each other, walk to Keawaiki, help each other drive the fishponds and lagoons, fish for *awa*. One of our projects when I was at Puʻuwaʻawaʻa was to make enough money for the kids' school equipment. We went to Kīholo and caught *awa* and mullet, and we made *kūlolo* (coconut-taro pudding) with taro from *ma uka* and had a huge sale." They made $3,500, Paris reports proudly, and purchased the first audiovisual equipment for the county's old Puʻuanahulu School.

*Annie 'Una, a tiny, spirited woman, is remembered by the kama'āina of Kekaha as the last Hawaiian resident of the Makalawena shoreline and one who used the* ma uka-to-ma kai *and coastline trails for everything from gathering salt to paying her respects at the death of a friend. Although most residents left the coast after the 1946 tsunami, 'Una remained in a house on stilts and raised goats, pigs, dogs, and chickens.* Photograph by Norman Carlson. Courtesy of Kona Historical Society.

*"My folks would put me on our horse. Just me,"* Agnes Haleʻamaʻu Ohira, then in her late eighties, told Hannah Springer in 1986. "Tie me to the saddle, send me *ma kai*. I would fall asleep. Ah, soon I would be leaving Kūkiʻo and on to Kaʻūpūlehu.... I would take the old folks *kalo* (taro). I would help with the evening chores.... The old man would bundle fish for me to take home. Before sunrise the next day, going ma uka. When that horse died, I never went back."[11]

Agnes Haleʻamaʻu Ohira traveled on the network of trails that for centuries was the lifeblood of Kekaha. All segments of the community depended on the trails as the only means of overland transportation. The trails enabled the natives to gather and share food and the materials needed for shelter, medical care, canoe building, rituals, and clothing.[12] Subsistence—survival—depended on them. But even with the use of donkeys (which arrived in Hawaiʻi in 1825 and also outlived their usefulness), travel across the lava lands remained difficult, and the fountain grass and mullein were propagating indiscriminately. Joe Makaʻai, one of the last surviving residents of Kaʻūpūlehu, recalls that it took an hour and a half to reach the doctor "up *ma uka*," and about two-and-a-half hours to get to Kohala on the narrow coastline trail. Except for the missionaries and chiefs—the privileged few who had early access to horseback travel—Kekaha's residents, like other Hawaiians, moved across the *ahupuaʻa* predominantly on foot until the 1830s. In the next decade, with the increasing use of horses and mules, the Hawaiians modified many of their foot trails by removing the smooth, slippery stones that were difficult for the animals to negotiate, or by adding curbstone borders to keep the saddlepack animals on the trail.[13]

Kahuwai Bay, where Makaʻai lived, a village called Makalawena, and Kīholo were in prime coastal locations that made them the crossroads for several trails: the south—north Kailua-to-Kawaihae trail, a trail that runs upslope to Huʻehuʻe, and others that lead to the agricultural and ranching areas of Puʻuwaʻawaʻa and Puʻuanahulu. In the first decade of the twentieth century, the fishing village of Makalawena had a church, school, store, and seven or eight houses, all of which were destroyed in the 1946 tsunami.[14] Residents raised goats, an important component of the regional economy at the turn of the century, and a large pond called Kapoʻikai teemed with the tiny red shrimp called

*Having navigated the* ma uka-to-ma kai *trail from Huʻehuʻe, John Avery Maguire and his party arrive at Kalaemanō, noted for its stores of salt, on their way to the beach at Kaʻūpūlehu, circa 1910.* Courtesy of Hannah Kihalani Springer.

*ʻōpaeʻula*, used as bait for *ʻōpelu* fishing. Movement across the *kaha* lands transected these villages and left trail remnants that can still be traveled, among them the *ma uka — ma kai* trail that ends near the southeastern corner of Makalawena's pond.

Hannah Springer recalls how these trails served her family in times of grief as well as joy. When her grandmother died in the uplands of Huʻehuʻe, it was the trails that carried the news and brought expressions of solace. "My grandmother died in the afternoon, and by ten o'clock the next morning, her dear friend Annie ʻUna could be seen and heard walking up the trail from Makalawena at the shore to Huʻehuʻe," Springer notes. "My mother and her sisters recalled how, before they saw Annie, they could hear her wailing in lament as she walked up the trail, and it sent shivers through them."

Springer also recounts the stories her mother and aunts passed on to her about their festive journeys from the uplands of Huʻehuʻe to Kūkiʻo at the coastline. With their horses "sliding down the cinder hill, Puʻuokai,"[15] they headed for the spring-laden Kūkiʻo with their initial supplies strapped on horse or mule. As the weeks went by, subsequent provisions would arrive from Kailua by boat. In such fashion did the *kamaʻāina* of the region enjoy the fruits of their long and arduous overland travel: with gracious, leisurely sojourns that allowed them the full and unhurried absorption of the pleasures they had labored to reach. In their long white dresses and wide-brimmed hats, the ladies of Huʻehuʻe, and the men in their white shirts and jaunty bandannas, sat astride in a sartorial elegance that contrasted sharply with the harshness of the terrain.

Modes of travel across the *ahupuaʻa* have changed with time and technology. Even with the earth-moving activity occurring in Kekaha today, there are still those who follow the coastal pathways of the ancients. Where possible, fishermen and water sports enthusiasts follow the old shoreline trails as they seek recreation and access to the ocean in their four-wheel drive vehicles. Springer's family is among the few who continue to use the *ma uka — ma kai* trail, as their forebears did before them, moving from uplands to shoreline and to favored spots in between, their senses alert to the shifting winds and fragile terrain of the dryland forest. Although Springer's husband, Michael Tomich, walks the five-mile distance from the coastline to Kukuiʻohiwai in an hour, more often than not they and other twentieth-century *kamaʻāina* make their journeys on sure-footed, four-wheel-drive vehicles that have replaced the horses slipping on cinder hills.

*The* wiliwili, *a dryland forest plant, is among those endangered by forest fires, grazing animals, and fountain grass. Wiliwili seeds are strung into elaborately patterned* lei *while the flowers in bloom, it is said, signify that sharks are mating. The lightness of* wiliwili *wood makes it ideal for canoe floats. In former times, when large trees were more abundant,* wiliwili *was the preferred wood for buoyant surfboards.*

For those who were able to enjoy it, ranching was good, clean outdoor living. But as an industry, it had a number of unintended repercussions. The lands of Kekaha are part of a fragile, complex ecosystem. Ranching encroached on this ecosystem and brought with it a unique set of environmental problems that are still being grappled with today. "It is in these peculiar regions that the botanical collector will find more in one day collecting than in a week or two in a wet region, and...it is indeed astonishing that these various places like Puuwaawaa, North Kona, Hawaii...have been entirely neglected by the botanical collectors who have previously visited these islands," wrote Joseph F. Rock in *The Indigenous Trees of the Hawaiian Islands,* first published in 1913. He called Puʻuwaʻa-waʻa "the richest floral section of any in the whole Territory" and said that at least sixty percent of all the species of indigenous trees growing in these islands could be found in areas such as Puʻuwaʻawaʻa.

Ranchers introduced into this ecosystem mullein and fountain grass for ground cover and silver oak and eucalyptus for timber and windbreaks, unaware that the species would one day imperil native plants. They had no way of knowing that these aggressive alien species would outpace and displace the precious native forests.

"When Grandpa John (Maguire) was a territorial forester, he experimented with silver oak and eucalyptus and other alien species," Springer explains. "He also experimented with native Hawaiian species for refor-

*Among the endangered species protected by federal and state regulations is* uhiuhi, *whose flowers, top right, are still seen occasionally in the forests of Kaʻūpūlehu. There are only 120* uhiuhi *trees remaining in Hawaiʻi's wilds. Hawaiians made fish spears, digging sticks, tapa beaters, and house posts out of* uhiuhi, *the heaviest of the native woods. Also an excellent native hardwood,* māmane *had similar uses and grows in elevations up to nine thousand feet. Forest birds feed on its flowers, right, which were also fashioned into* lei.

estation. But then, as now, the introduced species have faster growth rates. My grandfather made it a part of his will that his lands were to be used for agriculture and agricultural purposes only."

In the mid- and high-elevation forests, some rare and culturally significant native plants—*koa*, *'ōhi'a*, *uhiuhi*, *'ēlama* (native ebony), *kauila*, *halapepe*, *'aiea*, *māmane*, and *'iliahi*—began to disappear. The fragile native plants had to compete first with grazing animals, and then with the fountain grass that blanketed the landscape. The *'āina*, historically coveted and fought over by Hawaiian chiefs and warriors, was suddenly battling for its own survival. For centuries Hawaiians had used the plants for ritual offerings, to build houses and canoes, to store and carry food, and for a variety of other purposes. Now these culturally important plants were endangered.

Game management, like food production, was a challenge that never ceased. Goats continually sheared the landscape, eating the vegetation intended for cattle. As a young child, Billy Paris watched as his father and uncles participated in eradication campaigns, aiming at the goats from the back of a Model T truck with bullets provided by the government. "It was nothing to shoot seventy-five goats in an afternoon," he says. *Kama'āina* still recall the wild goat drives of the 1920s. The first, in 1922, began in Pu'uanahulu at about the 4,000-foot elevation. "They lined up the goats and drove them down below the highway and held them overnight," says Paris, who, although an infant at the time, learned about the goat drives as part of his family lore. "The next morning, the goats were driven down to Kīholo, where they were led to the peninsula between the lagoon and the ocean. The area was blocked off with wire. The people who wanted goat meat came to Kīholo on their horses. Then they slaughtered the goats and dried the meat, staying for a week." According to government reports, 7,000 wild goats[16] were exterminated. Five years later, a second goat drive claimed 7,500. According to Paris, for years after the goat drives concluded, domestic pigs waded across the lagoon entrance to pick off the residue from the carcasses. "And to this day, at the end of the lagoon, there's a mound of goat bones," he says.

Paris and his wife, Bertha, live in Kainaliu now, at the boundary between North and South Kona. Although he is pushing seventy-five in years, he remains the romantic image of the stalwart, hardworking Hawaiian cowboy, a testament to the salutary effects of the *paniolo* life. "I loved Puʻuwaʻawaʻa," he declares. "My wife says some of the happiest days of our lives were spent there. It's a healthy place to live, with everybody outdoors and the kids with rosy cheeks. They all had rosy cheeks. In the old days, you'd see them riding to school on horseback."

But for the most part, ranch life is a memory in Kekaha, and elders like Paris are among the few remaining scions of the industry. In 1958, the Hind family sold Puʻuwaʻawaʻa Ranch to Dillingham Investment Company, which later sold to Newell Bohnett. While part of the land remains in cattle ranching, the rest has been designated by the state as the Puʻuwaʻawaʻa Wildlife Sanctuary.

The sale of Huʻehuʻe Ranch by the Stillman Trust was finalized ten years later, although its dismantling came in stages. "From early on, the land holdings were not contiguous," explains Springer. "The most peripheral lands were sold first because the effort was always to protect the core of the ranch." Escalating taxes and maintenance costs contributed to the ranch's demise, she says, but "basically it was sold for foolish reasons, mostly to cover the families' debts and to cover their lavish lifestyle."

Springer is a prime cultural and environmental resource of Kekaha who lives with her family at the thirty-three-acre Kukuiʻohiwai, given to her grandparents as a wedding present. Although it was never operated as a part of Huʻehuʻe Ranch, Kukuiʻohiwai, with its family cemetery and guest log of visiting kings, queens, and honored neighbors, was its spiritual center and a model of hospitality from earliest times. And it remains so. Although Kukuiʻohiwai was protected from change, the view around it—a sweeping panorama of Springer's ancestral homelands—was altered, inevitably, with the sale of the ranch. While some of the acreage is still in ranch land, a golf course has gone in a mile away, and a subdivision is to come. At the shoreline, construction activity and equipment are visible.

In the rarefied upper regions of Hualalai, above Huʻehuʻe, Barbara and Garner Anthony of Hualalai Ranch have managed to evade the pitfalls that have forced most of the other large landowners to sell. In the late 1950s, Barbara Cox Anthony (who was ranked number fifteen in a 1993 *Fortune* magazine story on the "World's 101 Richest People")[17] and her husband were longtime visitors to the area, and were looking to buy. And they did. Lifelong ranchers with sprawling ranch lands in

*"Friends have gathered, eyes have met at Kukuʻiohiwai, all enjoying this place standing in the calm,"* wrote Haunani Apoliona in her award-winning song, "Kukuʻiohiwai." Kukuʻiohiwai was a wedding gift from rancher John Avery Maguire to his granddaughter, Aileen Maguire, and her husband, Arthur Stillman, whose descendants still live there. Hannah Kihalani Springer, her husband, Michael Tomich, and their children, Kekaulike and Thelma, are the present residents of Kukuʻiohiwai, described by Apoliona as *"This home encircled by* kukui *trees, these symbols that adorn the land of our elders."* Here Michael, Kekaulike, and Thelma Tomich enjoy one of their many outdoor activities.

California and Australia, they purchased the *ma uka* portion of the Kaʻūpūlehu lease to start Hualalai Ranch in 1961. A prominent environmentalist who serves on the board of the World Wildlife Fund, Barbara Anthony says they bought the ranch lands not only because of their affinity for the region, but also to protect them from development. To make the land habitable, the Anthonys built two reservoirs and crushed the volcanic cinder to make soil. Today there are three- to four-hundred head of Santa Gertrudis cattle, an extensive vegetable garden, eight houses on the property, a crew of ranch hands, four Labradors, a pet cemetery, and a climate and view unequaled in Hawaiʻi.

"I always loved Puʻuwaʻawaʻa, and this was the same kind of climate," Barbara Anthony explains. "It's not windy, it's very cool. I moved to Hawaiʻi in January of 1946 and was dying to stay in a place like this." From an elevation of 3,500 feet on the slopes of Hualalai, the view from the ranch embraces the entire coastline, from ʻUpolu Point in the north clear down to Keāhole. In between are the emerald-green *puʻu* of Waimea, the voluptuous hills of Puʻuwaʻawaʻa, the stark silhouette of Puhiapele, the lava fingers and *kīpuka*—the story of Kekaha, written in its landscape.

In some ways, the story of the ranches of Kekaha parallels the early history of

*Hualalai Ranch manager Franklin Boteilho, above, competes every other month in rodeo competitions and wins frequently. Top scores in calf roping, team roping, double mugging (simulating the wild cattle-roping of the vaqueros), and other skills won him the saddle for "All Around Cowboy" from the 1995 Honokaa Stampede. Richard Gourley, left, is responsible for the care, feeding, and branding of the three hundred Santa Gertrudis cattle of Hualalai Ranch. With him in front of the tack room is Gilbert Loando, a third-generation paniolo who has worked at the ranch for twenty-six years.*

Kaʻūpūlehu—without the bloodshed. In the ongoing saga of the region, Kekaha's ranching history remains tinged with the desire, ingenuity, and competition that have marked Kaʻūpūlehu from the time of Kamalālāwalu and the covetous chiefs of Maui. In the modern scenario, Bishop Estate is the reigning chief, and paper and money, not war, determine ownership.

Garner Anthony explains: "If you look at the pattern of ownership in the region, it has changed considerably in the past hundred years, with the exception of the Bishop Estate. A lot of the old families that had substantial holdings sold various parts of them. The Bishop Estate stands alone in that it hasn't sold any of its holdings. In fact, they've increased them." In 1959, the Anthonys, in search of a large tract of land, formed a group to acquire a lease from the Bishop Estate. "Our original group wasn't in any position to fulfill some of the conditions that Bishop Estate wanted fulfilled," he continues. "They wanted waterfront development, such as beachfront bungalows. To do even that was beyond our means." Just as Anthony's group, the Hualalai Development Corporation, began to search for a sub-tenant who could assume those burdens, an oilman named Johnno Jackson appeared.

He was an unforgettable character, a wildcatter with an uncanny instinct for drilling wells and finding gushers. The instincts that proved so successful in tapping oil on the mainland proved equally successful in finding water in the barren lavascape that was Kaʻūpūlehu. According to the Anthonys, Jackson wanted to develop Makalawena. But the sublease was not available, and in 1961 he settled for Kaʻūpūlehu. "We split the lease and were able to get Johnno Jackson to assume development of the *ma kai* portion of Kaʻūpūlehu," continues Garner Anthony. "The upper road (Māmalahoa Highway) was the dividing factor." While the Anthonys acquired the sublease for the 7,000-acre *ma uka* portion of the property, Jackson assumed the responsibility for developing sixty-two of the 11,000 acres in the *ma kai* portion of the *ahupuaʻa*. It was a match made, literally, in the heavens.

"There were no roads, so everything came in by boat," recalls Barbara Anthony. "We had a radio, so Johnno would radio me from Kaʻūpūlehu and ask me to telephone so-and-so. He worked so hard, but I honestly didn't think he'd get anything going." He did, and his masterpiece, the Kona Village Resort, was the opening act in a new era for Kaʻūpūlehu.

*New Horizons*

Overleaf — *The ponds of Ka'ūpūlehu, like this one near Waiakauhi, form oases of moisture in the* kaha *lands.*

*Honokōhau, the southern border of Kekaha, is recorded at its most idyllic in this painting by Lloyd Sexton. The Hilo-born artist immortalized many of North Kona's landmarks before he died in 1990 at seventy-eight years old.* Courtesy of Mr. and Mrs. Garner Anthony.

JOHNNO JACKSON'S X-ray vision saw gold in the baked black lava fields and thorny *kiawe* trees of Ka'ūpūlehu. Like the Hawaiian chiefs who prized these lands, who fought and even died for them, Jackson recognized the intrinsic value of the *'āina* long before it became the resort of his dreams and a worldwide symbol of iconoclastic luxury. Jackson, of Island Copra and Trading Company, was a man of instinct. When he swam and fished in the pristine waters and gazed at Hualalai in the distance, her hardened lava gracefully spilling from summit to the sea, he was moved by the power of Ka'ūpūlehu. "I'm going to build a resort here," he declared.

He did, and when he died in 1991, his ashes, like those of his first wife and many others, were scattered three-and-a-half miles offshore from the resort that he had manifested against all odds. Emerging in stages, the Kona Village had gained renown for its isolation, authenticity of Polynesian architecture, and uniquely unhurried pace. Jackson's acquisition of the land was just the beginning; the desolate landscape offered nothing resembling infrastructure—neither paved roads, running water, electricity, nor telephone lines. To build the resort of his dreams, Jackson had construction materials delivered in an amphibious landing craft purchased from U.S. military surplus. He also built a private, 2,600-foot landing strip in the middle of a lava field to complement the only access by land, a barely navigable Jeep trail.

Jackson was an oil man who had made high scores in finding gushers on the mainland, and it was this seasoned, intuitive gaze that he directed to the parched landscape of Ka'ūpūlehu. Despite its legendary stores of underground water and shoreline springs, Kekaha on its surface was dry and barren— *Kekaha Wai 'ole*. Fresh running water was an immediate requirement, and fortunately for Jackson, he could find it. "He went right up on a hill and said, 'I want to drill a well right here'," says Fred Duerr, Kona Village general manager who has worked at the resort almost since its inception. Jackson remained impervious to the chorus of protests claiming the spot was too close to the coastline. "All of a sudden, they're drilling a water well," Duerr recalls with delight. "It was the smallest producing water well in the state of Hawai'i. If he had moved a hundred feet in another direction, he probably wouldn't have found good water." But water did flow in the *kaha* lands; eventually Jackson found three wells for the Kona Village Resort.

Suddenly the barren lavascape became fertile ground for business interests. Those interests that followed Jackson to Ka'ūpūlehu were a re-casting of the warring chiefs who had competed for centuries over what historian Samuel Kamakau called the desirable "warm food and drinking water, and tough and tender fish" of Kona. In 1959, three years after Jackson first sailed along the Kona Coast with his wife, Helen, a Boeing 707, the first all-jet passenger plane to hit Hawai'i, landed at Honolulu International Airport. With it came a new era of tourism that fomented a reversal of traditional Hawaiian perspectives on land use and stewardship. With burgeoning waves of visitors streaming to the shores of Hawai'i, the pleasures of leisure, rather than the responsibilities of subsistence, became a prevailing concern. Development of land was a major vehicle for these new priorities. Land, the entity that had always fed and sustained the Hawaiians, became a gleam in the speculator's eye, a modern income-producing commodity desired as much by developers as by the chiefs of old. And Kekaha, with its warm weather, *aku*-laden leeward waters, sunset ambiance, wetlands, fishponds, and unparalleled mountain views, possessed an allure that became more compelling with time—and an environment far more fragile than anticipated.

Jackson, with the sublease he acquired from Hualalai Development in 1961, began building on sixty-two acres at the shoreline of Ka'ūpūlehu, on the bay called Kahuwai where the Waters of Kāne bubbled freely. The Kona Village opened on December 23, 1965, with thatched cottages, called *hale*, built in the architectural styles of Hawai'i, Samoa, Tahiti, Fiji, and the Marquesas Islands. Over the course of the next thirty years, the resort expanded from its original fifty *hale* to a hundred-twenty-five *hale* scattered over eighty-two acres.

Not long after it opened, Jackson sold Kona Village to Signal Oil and Gas, a company with which he had worked in California. The sale of the resort marked the beginning of a significant presence for Signal in Hawai'i and a long history of land transactions reflecting the growing appeal of West Hawai'i. As part of the deal, Signal bought the Hualalai Development Corporation,[1] whose principal asset was the sixty-five-year master lease on the entire parcel. At the same time, the Garner Anthonys of Hualalai Development Corporation acquired a new sublease on the 7,000-acre *ma uka* portion, thereby continuing what has become uninterrupted tenure of the upper lands. Eventually the Anthonys, for tax reasons, sold their sublease to Cox Enterprises, a privately held company owned by Mrs.

Anthony and her sister. The sublessee of the *ma uka* portion is now a company called the Hualalai Land Corporation, solely owned by Cox Enterprises of Atlanta. In addition to landowner Bishop Estate, this corporation has turned out to be the most enduring player in the ever-changing Ka'ūpūlehu landscape.

After investing in the Kona Village Resort, Signal continued to look for other places to put its money and began buying up land—a lot of it. Bob McIntosh, who worked for Signal from 1969 until he retired in 1989 as president,[2] says the company eventually acquired some 54,000 acres. Stretching from South Kohala to Kona, Signal's holdings included 36,000 acres of fee simple property and 18,000 acres leased at Ka'ūpūlehu from the Bishop Estate. In subsequent years, as they systematically sold their holdings, Signal's presence in the area waned; the void was quickly filled by new businesses prospecting for gold in the plains of Kekaha.

The ensuing land transactions were exceedingly complex, with a changing cast of characters. In and around Kekaha, a new frontier for modern hospitality, several notable influences converged in the sixties and seventies and foreshadowed the new era. In 1965, Laurance Rockefeller's Mauna Kea Beach Hotel opened in Kawaihae, north of Kekaha, and staked its claim as a tranquil hideaway for sophisticated travelers. Then came the Kona Village later that year, a low-key presence that grew in renown as each thatched *hale* sprouted from the lava in a celebration of innocent Polynesia. Elsewhere in Hawai'i, the future zoomed closer in the master-planned resorts unveiled for Kā'anapali and Wailea on Maui. South of Kailua on Hawai'i island,

Bishop Estate unveiled ambitious plans for a master-planned community at Keauhou-Kona that included hotels, homes, a golf course, and commercial space. Hospitality, a quality innately abundant in the Hawaiian people, was suddenly being transformed into a business and an art form, the western coastline of Hawai'i its fertile ground.

In small but significant increments, resort development opened up access to the region. In 1970, commercial airline carriers were landing apace at the new Keāhole Airport in Kona, unloading waves of travelers. Five years later, in 1975, a long, straight throughway called the Queen Ka'ahumanu Highway—Highway 19—cut through the *'a'ā* and *pāhoehoe*, creating a fast, easy connecting link between Kailua and Puakō. By the time the Sheraton Royal Waikoloan opened in 'Anaeho'omalu in 1980 with its five-hundred-plus rooms, followed by the Mauna Lani Resort three years later, the desirable *kaha* lands were a growing mecca of hospitality and leisure.

"The Ka'ahumanu Highway completely opened that shoreline in West Hawai'i," recalls Garner Anthony of Hualalai Ranch, who, with his wife, used to toil for hours over primitive, gut-wrenching Jeep trails to deliver wine and merriment on their visits to Annie 'Una, the last Hawaiian resident of Makalawena. "Before that, the feasibility of any large-scale development in the *ma kai* area was impossible, because there was no suitable access."

Not surprisingly, Ka'ūpūlehu was a microcosm for the speculation boom. It possessed a colorful history and a strong sense of place that had remained inviolable through the centuries. In the stark lava fields of Ka'ūpūlehu, a new mix was brewing that would meld a *malihini* community with *kamaʻāina*, modernity with the spirit of the ancients.

In 1979 Cambridge Pacific, a Canadian company, acquired the Kona Village as well as Signal's lease for Kaʻūpūlehu. But unable to pay its bill for drilling water, Cambridge went into partnership in 1984 with Barnwell Hawaiian Properties. The subsidiary they formed developed the first master plan for Kaʻūpūlehu, which was approved two years later, in 1986.

The plan called for a 600-acre development encompassing two golf courses, two hotels, and a residential community. In spite of its lofty goals, the plan turned out to be incompatible with the low-key flavor of leisure and hospitality for which Kaʻūpūlehu was historically known. While the master plan was brewing, more changes were in store for the Kona Village. It was sold to a company called AIRCOA (Associated Inns & Resorts Company of America) but after four years changed hands again, to present owner Kona Village Associates.

In the late eighties, demand for the *kaha* lands reached fever pitch as a colorful new wave of North American and Japanese investors began appearing on the parched plains of Kaʻūpūlehu. They had big dreams, brought large infusions of cash to the region, took risks, and sometimes failed. One by one they came: IDG, whose golf- and sports-oriented concept attracted the Four Seasons; Princess Hotels, which wanted to build a six-story, 600-room hotel but eventually dropped the idea; Potomac Investment Associates (PIA), which took charge of the residential development; and Cosmo World, which hoped to link Kaʻūpūlehu to a glamorous coterie of international golf clubs. In particular, IDG and PIA were speculators attracted by the opportunity to capitalize on the Japanese bubble economy that was making its mark in Hawaiʻi.

If Cosmo World's dream had materialized, Kaʻūpūlehu would have become a sister resort to Pebble Beach Golf Links, dubbed the "Sistine Chapel of golf" and "an American shrine" by golf great Jack Nicklaus and others. Minoru Isutani, chairman of Cosmo World, bought out IDG and Princess Hotels in 1989 to become owner of Kaʻūpūlehu's planned resort. Hoping to create a string of tony golf resorts around the world, he then plunked down $841 million to buy the Pebble Beach Golf Links in California. Eighteen months later, in January of 1992, he sold his trophy course for $574 million,[3] a victim of the Persian Gulf crisis and the plummeting Japanese stock market. His ultimate undoing, however, was a ruling by the California Coastal Commission, which rejected his plans to privatize the legendary links.

Instead of becoming a sister resort to Pebble Beach Golf Links, as Cosmo World had hoped, Kaʻūpūlehu's planned resort moved in fits and spurts and eventually languished—not for months, but for years. The Persian Gulf War, an international economic slowdown, and the collapse of the Japanese bubble pulled the curtain on the go-go years, and the project ground to a halt in mid-air. Shooting out of the stark lavascape amid the plains and *puʻu* of Kaʻūpūlehu was a partially built three-story elevator shaft, attached to a two-story hotel building. The structure pierced the horizon like a spear through the heart of the land. The only edifice visible for miles in all directions, a ghost of its former owners, it baked for three years in the searing Kaʻūpūlehu sun, abandoned by failed investors. In the summer of 1992, while heat waves radiated from the lava and distorted the silhouette of the half-built blight, Kajima Corporation, which was Cosmo World's general contractor, took over the Kaʻūpūlehu project as controlling partner. During the following year, Hualalai Development Company was formed to manage the development, and in December, enlivened by a fresh new design and concept, Hualalai Development Company, to the delight of the West Hawaiʻi community, razed the inappropriate structure.

Thus were sown the seeds for a new community and a bold new beginning for an ancient place called Kaʻūpūlehu. The new concept of the Hualalai Development Company called for a seaside village of unobtrusive low-rise buildings containing a hotel, Four Seasons Resort Hawaii at Hualalai; an 18-hole Jack Nicklaus golf course, the Hualalai Golf Club; and a residential community that would inhabit a twenty-first-century version of the time-tested *ahupuaʻa*. In this new village, called Hualalai, the unique sense of place and the region's singular history would be celebrated from *ma uka* to *ma kai*.

Under the silent gaze of Hualalai, the mother mountain of Kona, the old footpaths cling to a terrain that grows increasingly fragile with time. Many generations have walked this land since the gods Kū and Hina received the humble prayers of the hopeful at the summit called Hainoa. The new era has brought new challenges, and with them come responsibilities that cannot be separated by the stone boundaries of an *ahupuaʻa*. In a reversal of historic times, when the resources of the *ʻāina* seemed a cornucopia of food and sustenance, it is Kekaha's plains, ponds, forests, and *puʻu* that require protection today.

Two centuries ago, Kamehameha lost his fishpond at Pāʻaiea to the wrathful fires of Pele. Although Hualalai seems at rest today, the plains and forests of Kekaha are still ablaze. Fueled by fountain grass and unseasonably dry weather conditions, forest fires in Kekaha torch the landscape every few years to claim a precious share of the *ʻāina*. The list reads like an obituary: thirty-one thousand acres in Puʻuanahulu in the 1970s; in 1992, ten acres of the last undamaged habitat for the endangered *kokiʻo*, *uhiuhi*, and *kauila*; in 1993, three-hundred-fifty acres of *ēlama* and *kauila* forest in the *kīpuka* called ʻŌweʻōwe at the upland border of Kaʻūpūlehu and Puʻuwaʻawaʻa; most recently, in March of 1995, twelve hundred acres on the slopes of Hualalai, including a thousand acres belonging to the Puʻuwaʻawaʻa Wildlife Sanctuary created to protect the Hawaiian crow, *ʻalalā*.

Out of the loss of habitat, out of the ashes of the native forests, has risen an enormous vigor and a new purpose that will chart Kekaha's future. Used by the ancients for vessels, implements, shelter, and rituals, the native woods charred by the fires have been gathered and partially distributed to a handful of native Hawaiian groups seeking them for traditional uses. Landowner Bishop Estate has stored the rest of the native wood, hopefully for gradual dispensation to future generations of native Hawaiians. *Hahai pono*—pursue righteousness—is the clarion call of the many tireless citizens' groups that find themselves empowered

*Heather and Bill Cole and their daughter, Shelley, spend their weekends watering, clearing fountain grass, and tending to the delicate native plants in the dryland forests of Ka'ūpūlehu, nearly two thousand feet high on Hualalai. They also erect signs and exclosures to help protect the* kauila, uhiuhi, koki'o, *and* 'ēlama *whose survival is threatened by fire and alien plants.*

with a renewed, and urgent, sense of stewardship. On weekends, in the quiet splendor of 'Owē'owē, a few concerned families from the region haul buckets of water to nurse the *kauila, uhiuhi, 'ēlama,* and *koki'o* that struggle to regenerate in their two-and-a-half acres of exclosures. Water trickles downhill through plastic hoses to moisten the parched soil. The signs, engaging onlookers in the responsibility, explain politely that the plants are endangered and in need of protection.

One of the caretakers of this fragile piece of *'āina* is Heather Cole, a full-time employee of the Hualalai Development Company, which encourages these environmental protection efforts. Cole and Roger Harris are the two consultants hired by PIA-Kona, a limited partnership that leases, from the Bishop Estate, eight thousand acres between Queen Ka'ahumanu and Māmalahoa highways.

Cole sees fountain grass as the region's major environmental threat because of its incendiary tendencies. In 1993, the Bishop Estate addressed this concern by financing the construction of a more than $30,000, mile-and-a-half graded firebreak road that encircles a portion of the vulnerable hillside, from Hu'ehu'e to the edge of the Ka'ūpūlehu lava flow. The firebreak protects the precious *kauila, uhiuhi, 'ōhi'a,* and other precious native trees that cling precariously to the hillside. The firebreak was one of the Bishop Estate's more prominent acts of stewardship. When a devastating 1993 fire decimated another, unprotected section of the dryland forest, it underscored the importance of fire prevention.

In and around Kona, concerned groups of citizens, and *malihini* too, have formed new and vigilant communities that promise to protect the native culture as well as the *'āina.* These groups seek to preserve access for traditional practices such as salt-gathering, fishing, and religion, and to guard against violations of environmental policy. It is not always smooth sailing, but hopes remain high. At the Ka'ūpūlehu seashore, the brilliant yellow-orange *kauna'oa* (dodder) is planted and nurtured around Waiakauhi Pond, where blankets of *pōhinahina,* a native beach shrub, *pōhuehue,* the indigenous beach morning glory, and the native sunflower called *nehe* cover the ground like blue-and-green velvet. *'Ōpae'ula* still swarm in the pond, as they did in Joe Maka'ai's youth. On moonless nights, from their sandy depths, the delicious black shells called *kūpe'e* appear at the shoreline, as they have since the beginning. The *'Eka* and *Ho'olua* still rustle through the bullrushes, the *'Ōlauniu* still pierces the coconut fronds. The fragile chirp of the wandering tattler, *'ūlili,* penetrates the dawn with a promise to return next winter. Seaward, the glorious sunset greets the gaze but remains a symbol that belongs to the horizon. Awash in a golden glow, the landmarks of Ka'ūpūlehu belong to her alone: the double-domed Kū'ili, the silver-black rivers of *pāhoehoe,* the *pu'u,* trails, ponds, shoreline, the distant stands of *'ōhi'a* and *kauila.* From the summit, her slopes sweeping to the sea in a silent embrace, Hualalai keeps her vigil.

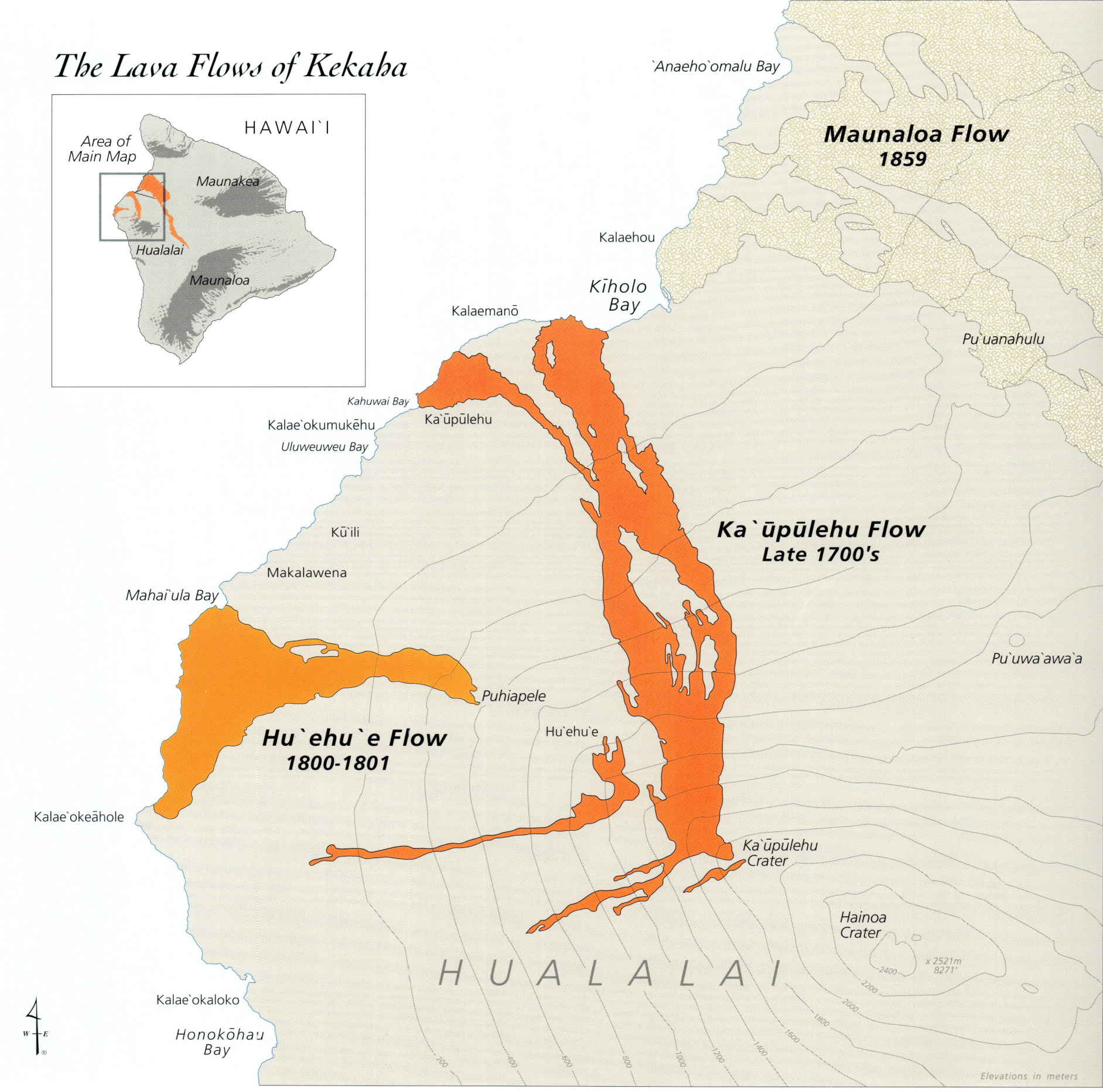

# Notes

### Pele's Wrath — Pages 42–61

1. Westervelt also wrote that there may have been forty sisters in Pele's family.
2. According to Joe Makaʻai, there are two separate sites in the uplands because each sister had her own dwelling.
3. Billy Paris further suggests that Kaʻimupūlehu can be broken down into *imu*, the underground oven, and *pūlehu*, to broil on hot coals. Although the two words appear contradictory, he says, it's conceivable that something placed on top of an *imu* will broil and sizzle, as in *pūlehu*, until covered.
4. The Papers of John Reinecke, Bishop Museum Archives.
5. Ibid.
6. In Joe Makaʻai's version, it was a lazy *menehune* who feigned a rooster's crowing so he wouldn't have to work.
7. Also called Waiakuhi Pond.
8. Old-timers like Makaʻai remember it as Kahuawai Bay.

### Blood and Bureaucracy — Pages 62–81

1. Some historians claim that Kamehameha received only custody of the war god, without the lands.
2. It was at Kealakekua Bay that, eleven years earlier, in a series of provocations by both foreigners and natives over a stolen boat, Captain James Cook was killed by natives.
3. Kameʻeleihiwa, Lilikalā. *Native Land and Foreign Desires*. Honolulu: Bishop Museum Press, 1992, p. 331.
4. Ibid, p. 130.
5. Kelly, Marion. *Kekaha: ʻĀina Maloʻo*. Honolulu: Bernice P. Bishop Museum, 1971, p. 7.
6. Kameʻeleihiwa, *Native Land and Foreign Desires*, p. 310.

### Astride on the Kaha Lands — Pages 82–103

1. Joe Makaʻai, personal interview.
2. Ibid.
3. Pukui, Mary Kawena. *ʻŌlelo Noʻeau*. Honolulu: Bishop Museum Press, 1983, p. 271
4. In the Big Island's North Kona and Kohala districts, four ranches—Huʻehuʻe, Puʻuwaʻawaʻa, Kahuā, and Parker Ranch—were owned by cousins who were the part-Hawaiian descendants of John Parker.
5. Kelly, Marion. *Kekaha: ʻĀina Maloʻo*, p. 13.
6. Larry Kimura, personal correspondence.
7. Maguire's second wife was Eliza Low, a schoolteacher and the author of *Kona Legends*, and the sister of Eben and Hannah Low.
8. Jean Greenwell's notes, Kona Historical Society.
9. According to Larry Kimura, Hannah Hind, the wife of Puʻuwaʻawaʻa founder Robert Hind, may have planted the first *kiawe* tree at Kīholo; from there it spread toward Kawaihae and south toward Keāhole.
10. Kona Historical Society notes.
11. Springer, Hannah. *Regional Notes from Kekaha: Kaʻupulehu*. Kukuiʻohiwai, Kaʻupulehu, 1989, p. 27.
12. State of Hawaiʻi Department of Land and Natural Resources. *Historic Trails of Hawaiʻi 1992*.
13. Ibid.
14. Kelly, Marion. *Appendix B: Historical Background of Kekaha, North Kona*. Honolulu: Department of Anthropology, Bernice Pauahi Bishop Museum, July 1973, p. 103.
15. Springer. *Regional Notes*, p. 27.
16. Tomich, Quentin. *Mammals in Hawaiʻi*. Honolulu: Bishop Museum Press, 1986, p. 152.
17. The magazine listed Anthony's worth at $5.8 billion along with her sister, Anne Cox Chambers, with whom she owns the Atlanta-based Cox Enterprises, a media company that owns newspapers, television, radio, cable TV, automobile auctions, and other interests.

### New Horizons — Pages 104–113

1. A group of shareholders of which Garner and Barbara Anthony are members; not to be confused with Hualalai Development Company, formerly Kaupulehu Land Company.
2. McIntosh was also president of Hualalai Development Corporation and Island Copra, Inc., which was doing business as Kona Village Resort.
3. Johnson, William Oscar. "Nature's Trophy." *Sports Illustrated*, June 22, 1992, page 85.

# Glossary

| | |
|---|---|
| ʻaʻā | rough, crumbly lava |
| ʻaʻaliʻi | indigenous shrub with a sturdy wood used in bait sticks, posts, and rafters; *Dodonaea viscosa* |
| Aʻe | northeast tradewind |
| ʻahi | Hawaiian tuna fishes, especially the yellowfin tuna |
| ahu | heap; rocks piled into an altar |
| ahupuaʻa | traditional Hawaiian land division, usually wedge-shaped and extending from mountain to sea |
| ʻaiea | the endemic Hawaiian genus *Nothocestrum*, in the nightshade family of soft-wooded shrubs or small trees |
| ʻāina | land, or pieces of land |
| ʻāina hānau | birthplace; ancestral lands |
| aku | bonito; skipjack tuna |
| akule | big-eyed scad fish |
| ʻalalā | Hawaiian crow |
| alia | a command to halt |
| aliʻi | chief or chiefess; royalty |
| ana huna | secret, hidden cave |
| ana wai | water cave |
| ʻapapane | Hawaiian honeycreeper |
| ʻaumakua | family or personal god; spirit guardian |
| ʻawa | kava, a Pacific Island native and shrub of the pepper family whose root is used to make a ceremonial and medicinal drink |
| ʻEka | the wind of Kona that sets up big sails for fishing |
| ʻēlama | *lama*, a native ebony; *Diospyros* |
| hahai pono | pursue well; *hahai i ka pono* — pursue righteousness |
| hala | screw pine, whose fronds are woven into mats, baskets, etc.; *Pandanus tectorius* |
| halapepe | Hawaiian dracaena, endemic member of the agave family; *Pleomele* |
| hale | house; building |
| haole | foreigner |
| hau | a Polynesian tree, member of the mallow family; *Hibiscus tiliaceus* |
| heiau | pre-Christian place of worship |
| holokū | loose dress with a train and usually a yoke, introduced by the missionaries |
| holomuʻu | a long, fitted dress, a combination of *holokū* and *muʻumuʻu* |
| hōlua | Hawaiian sled |
| Hoʻolua | strong north wind |
| huamoa | a variety of sweet potato |
| Hulumano | sudden, warm wind in Kona |
| ʻiʻiwi | scarlet-colored Hawaiian honeycreeper |
| ʻiliahi | Hawaiian sandalwood; *Santalum* |
| ʻiliʻili | small stones; pebbles |
| imu | underground oven |
| ipu | bottle gourd |
| kaha | hot, dry lands |
| kahuna | priest; minster; expert in a profession |
| kalo | taro; *Colocasia esculenta* |
| kamaʻāina | native-born |
| kaona | hidden meaning; concealed reference |
| kapa | tapa, the Hawaiian bark cloth |
| kapu | taboo |
| kauila | a dense native hardwood used in weapons, tools, implements; *Alphitonia ponderosa*; *Colubrina oppositifolia* |
| kaulana wai | place where water rests |
| Kaumuku | wind squall; a gusty afternoon wind sweeping down the slopes of Lālāmilo to the shore between Puakō and Kūkiʻo |
| kaunaʻoa | endemic dodder; *Cuscuta sandwichiana* |
| kiawe | algaroba tree; mesquite; *Prosopis pallida* |
| kīpuka | variation or change of form; clear place or oasis in a lava bed where there may be vegetation |
| koa | *acacia koa*, the largest of native forest trees, with light-gray bark, crescent-shaped leaves, and wood valued as lumber for canoes, surfboards, and calabashes |
| kohola | reef flats |
| kokiʻo | native shrubby hibiscus with red flowers; *Kokia* |
| kole | surgeonfish |
| konohiki | the head overseer of an *ahupuaʻa*; land steward |

| | | | |
|---|---|---|---|
| *koʻokoʻolau* | endemic herb or shrub used medicinally in tea; *Bidens* | *ʻōhiʻa* | a highly variable native Hawaiian tree; *Metrosideros polymorpha* |
| *kou* | tree valued for its wood, used to make calabashes and dishes; *Cordia subcordata* | *ʻŌlauniu* | a coconut-leaf-piercing wind renowned in Kekaha, Hawaiʻi |
| *Kūhonua* | infrequent but very strong wind that sweeps through North Kona, down the slopes of Hualalai | *ōʻō* | endemic, extinct black honey-eater |
| | | *ʻōpae* | shrimp |
| | | *ʻōpaeʻula* | small, reddish shrimp used for *ʻōpelu* bait |
| *kukui* | candlenut tree; *Aleurites moluccana* | *ʻōpelu* | mackerel scad |
| *kūlolo* | pudding made of taro and grated coconut, baked or steamed | *pāhoehoe* | smooth, black, shiny lava |
| | | *paʻiʻai* | hard, slightly pounded taro |
| *kulu wai* | water that drips, as in rock outcroppings in caves | *palu* | fish chum |
| | | *paniolo* | cowboy |
| *kūpeʻe* | anklet; edible shellfish (*Nerita polita*) | *pao wai* | dug-out pits |
| *kūpuna* | (plural form with macron, singular form without): grandparents; ancestors; elders | *pili* | indigenous Hawaiian grass used as thatch; *Heteropogon contortus* |
| *lānai* | porch; veranda | *pōhaku* | rock; stone; mineral |
| *lau hala* | pandanus leaves | *pōhinahina* | indigenous Hawaiian beach shrub; *Vitex rotundifolia* |
| *lehua* | flower of the *ʻōhiʻa* tree | | |
| *lepa* | banner; tapa cloth on the end of a stick, to mark a taboo area | *pōhuehue* | indigenous Hawaiian beach morning glory; *Ipomoea pes-caprae* |
| *loulu* | all species of native fan palms; *Pritchardia* | *poi* | a Hawaiian staple made of cooked taro pounded into a paste |
| *māhele* | portion; division; department | *pono* | goodness; righteousness |
| *makahiki* | year; annual; ancient festival of sports and religious observance lasting four months, beginning in October | *puaʻa* | pig |
| | | *puʻe* | a hill of sweet potatoes |
| | | *puhi* | to burn or set on fire |
| *ma kai* | toward the sea | *pūkiawe* | native shrub used medicinally; *Styphelia tameiameiae* |
| *malihini* | newcomer | | |
| *māmane* | endemic member of the pea family which thrives at high altitudes; *Sophora chrysophylla* | *pūlehu* | to broil |
| | | *pūʻolo* | bundle, bag, or container |
| | | *puʻu* | hill; peak; mound |
| *mamo* | black Hawaiian honeycreeper | *ʻuhane* | soul; spirit |
| *mana* | spiritual power | *uhiuhi* | an endemic legume with hard wood that was used in sleds, spears, and digging sticks; *Caesalpinia kavaiensis* |
| *manini* | very common reef surgeonfish, striped | | |
| *manuahi* | bird of fire; gratis | | |
| *ma uka* | toward the mountain | *uhu* | parrot fish |
| *menehune* | legendary race of small people who worked at night building ponds, roads, and temples | *ʻulu* | breadfruit; *Artocarpus altilis* |
| | | *ʻumeke* | bowl; calabash; circular vessel |
| | | *wai* | water; wealth |
| *Mumuku* | name of a strong wind at Kawaihae; same as Kaumuku | *wai ʻole* | dry; without water; barren |
| | | *wao akua* | mountainous region believed to be inhabited by gods and spirits; wilderness |
| *Nāulu* | name of a sudden, sweeping shower; a showery wind | *wiliwili* | endemic leguminous tree with very light wood; *Erythrina sandwicensis* |
| *nehe* | native shrubs and herbs in the daisy family; *Lipochaeta* | | |
| *nēnē* | Hawaiian goose | | |

# Bibliography

Armstrong, R. Warwick, editor and project director. *Atlas of Hawaii*. Honolulu: University of Hawai'i Press, 1983.

Beckwith, Martha. *Hawaiian Mythology*. Honolulu: University of Hawai'i Press, 1970.

Bird, Isabella. *Six Months in the Sandwich Islands*. Tokyo: Charles E. Tuttle Co., Inc., 1974.

Bowser, George. *The Hawaiian Kingdom Statistical and Commercial Directory and Tourist's Guide (Polk's Directory)*. Honolulu: Polk, 1880.

Carter, Laura. *An Archaeological Reconnaissance of the Makai Parcel of Ka'upulehu Ahupua'a, North Kona, Hawaii Island*. Honolulu: Department of Anthropology, Bernice Pauahi Bishop Museum, 1985.

Clark, John R. K. *Beaches of the Big Island*. Honolulu: University of Hawai'i Press, 1985.

Daws, Gavan. *Hawaii: The Islands of Life*. Honolulu: Signature Publishing, 1988.

Ellis, William. *Polynesian Researches: Hawaii*. Rutland, Vermont: Charles E. Tuttle Co., Inc., 1969.

Emerson, Nathaniel B. *Pele and Hiiaka: A Myth from Hawaii*. Tokyo: Charles E. Tuttle Co., Inc., 1978.

Emory, Kenneth, and Lloyd J. Soehren. *Archaeological and Historical Survey, Honokohau Area, North Kona, Hawaii*. Honolulu: Department of Anthropology, Bernice Pauahi Bishop Museum, 1971.

Johnson, William Oscar. "Nature's Trophy." *Sports Illustrated*, June 22, 1992, p. 68.

Handy, E. S. Craighill, and Elizabeth Green Handy. *Native Planters in Old Hawaii: Their Life, Lore, and Environment*. Honolulu: Bishop Museum Press, 1972.

Handy, E. S. Craighill, and Mary Kawena Pukui. *The Polynesian Family System in Ka-'u, Hawai'i*. Rutland, Vermont, & Tokyo, Japan: Charles E. Tuttle Co., Inc., 1972.

Ii, John Papa. *Fragments of Hawaiian History*. Honolulu: Bernice Pauahi Bishop Museum, 1959.

Kaakua, J. H. *Ka Hae Hawaii*, Nov. 9, 1859 (translated by Mary Kawena Pukui).

Kalākaua, David. *The Legends and Myths of Hawaii*. Rutland, Vermont, and Tokyo, Japan: Charles E. Tuttle Co., Inc., 1972.

Kalima, Lehua. "Appendix B: Historical Documentary Research," *Archaeological Inventory Survey, Ka'upulehu Mauka Lands Golf Course II Area and Remaining Area*, Susan T. Goodfellow and James Head, Land of Ka'upulehu, North Kona District, Island of Hawaii, PHRI, September 1992.

Kalima, Lehua. "Appendix B: Historical Documentary Research," *Archaeological Inventory Survey, Ka'upulehu Mauka Lands Project Area*, Susan T. Goodfellow, James Head, and Paul Rosendahl, Land of Ka'upulehu, North Kona District, Island of Hawaii, PHRI, March 1991.

Kamakau, Samuel M. *Ruling Chiefs of Hawaii*, revised edition. Honolulu: Kamehameha Schools/Bishop Estate, 1992.

Kamakau, Samuel M. *The People of Old: Ka Po'e Kahiko*. Honolulu: Bishop Museum Press, 1964.

Kamakau, Samuel M. *The Works of the People of Old*. Honolulu: Bishop Museum Press, 1976.

Kame'eleihiwa, Lilikalā. *Native Land and Foreign Desires: Pehea Lā E Pono Ai?* Honolulu: Bishop Museum Press, 1992.

Kane, Herb. *Voyagers*. Bellevue, Washington: WhaleSong, Incorporated, 1991.

Kawaharada, Dennis, editor. *Hawaiian Fishing Legends*. Honolulu: Kalamaku Press, 1992.

Kelly, Marion. "Appendix B: Historical Background of Kekaha, North Kona," *Archaeological Salvage of the Ke-ahole to Anaehoomalu Section of the Kailua-Kawaihae Road (Queen Kaahumanu Highway), Island of Hawaii*, Paul Rosendahl. Honolulu: Department Of Anthropology, Bernice Pauahi Bishop Museum, July 1973.

Kelly, Marion. "Appendix C: Notes on the History of Ka'upulehu," *Archaeological Inventory Survey, Ka'upulehu Mauka Lands Golf Course II Area and Remaining Area*, Susan T. Goodfellow, James Head, and Paul Rosendahl, Land of Ka'upulehu, North Kona District, Island of Hawaii, PHRI, March 1991.

Kelly, Marion. *Kekaha: 'Aina Malo'o*. Honolulu: Department of Anthropology, Bernice Pauahi Bishop Museum, 1971.

Kona Historical Society, *Ka Huaka'i I Kuki'o*, March 1986.

*Laws of the Republic of Hawaii*. Special Session, 1895.

Legislative Reference Bureau. *Public Land Policy in Hawaii: An Historical Analysis*. Honolulu: University of Hawai'i, Legislative Reference Bureau Report No. 5, 1969.

MacKenzie, Melody Kapilialoha, editor. *Native Hawaiian Rights Handbook.* Honolulu: Native Hawaiian Legal Corporation, 1991.

Maguire, Eliza D. *Kona Legends*. Hawaii: Petroglyph Press, 1966.

Malo, David. *Hawaiian Antiquities,* translated from the Hawaiian by Dr. Nathaniel B. Emerson, 1898. Honolulu: Bishop Museum Press, 1951.

Maly, Kepā. "Appendix C: Historical Documentary Research (Report 1397-112593)," *Archaeological Inventory Survey, Ka'ūpūlehu Makai Lot 4,* by Paul H. Rosendahl, Nov. 25, 1993.

Martin, Lynn, editor and project director. *Na Paniolo o Hawai'i.* Honolulu: Honolulu Academy of Arts, 1987.

Moore, Richard B., David Clague, Meyer Rubin, and Wendy A. Bohrson. "Volcanism in Hawaii," Chapter 20, United States Geological Survey Professional Paper 1350.

Nakuina, Moses K. *The Wind Gourd of La'amaomao,* translated by Esther T. Mookini and Sarah Nakoa. Honolulu: Kalamaku Press, 1992.

Pukui, Mary Kawena, and Samuel H. Elbert. *Hawaiian Dictionary*. Honolulu: University of Hawai'i Press, 1981.

Pukui, Mary Kawena, Samuel H. Elbert, and Esther T. Mookini. *Place Names of Hawaii*. Honolulu: University Press of Hawai'i, 1974.

Reinecke, John. The Papers of John Reinecke, Bishop Museum Archives.

Renger, Robert. *Archaeological Reconnaissance of Coastal Kaloko and Kuki'o, North Kona, Hawaii.* Honolulu: Department of Anthropology, Bernice Pauahi Bishop Museum, November 1970.

Rock, Joseph F. *The Indigenous Trees of the Hawaiian Islands.* Rutland, Vermont, & Tokyo, Japan: Charles E. Tuttle Co., Inc., 1974.

Soehren, Lloyd J. *Archaeology and History in Ka'upulehu and Makalawena, Kona, Hawaii.* Honolulu: Bernice Pauahi Bishop Museum, April 1963.

Springer, Hannah. *Regional Notes from Kekaha: Ka'upulehu.* Kekaha: Ka'upulehu Ma Uka Conservation and Agricultural Lands, November 1989.

Stearns, Harold T., and Gordon A. MacDonald. *Geology and Ground-Water Resources of the Island of Hawaii.* Honolulu: Geological Survey, United States Department of the Interior, 1946.

Titcomb, Margaret. *Native Use of Fish in Hawaii.* Honolulu: University Press of Hawai'i, 1972.

# Acknowledgments

Many people assisted in the preparation of this book. Some of them lived generations ago, others continue their traditions and enable efforts like this to go forth. I thank all of them, living and departed.

I am deeply grateful for the friendship and generosity of Hannah Kihalani Springer, who housed us, hosted us, and advised us. It is her voice that rings clearly through these stories of her homeland. Joe Maka'ai, Billy Paris, and Carol Leina'ala Lightner were also invaluable in piecing together the rich history of the region. In sharing their stories of Kekaha, they unite us with times and voices that would otherwise be buried in the crush of modernity. For enriching our lives in this way, my deepest appreciation is extended to the *kama'āina* of Kona.

I am also indebted to the stalwart souls who answered my unrelenting requests and queries: Jean Greenwell, Una Greenaway, and others at the Kona Historical Society; photographer Wayne Levin; Lynn Kau and Victoria Nihi at the Hawai'i State Archives; Luella Holt Kurkjian, Betty Lou Kam, DeSoto Brown, Stewart W. H. Ching, and Marge Kemp at the Bishop Museum Archives. I wish also to thank those at the Kamehameha Schools/Bishop Estate office in Kona, who granted us the access that produced some of this book's most stunning photographs.

Thank you to Grady Timmons, a peerless friend and editor who triumphed over a difficult manuscript; to Larry Kimura, for his meticulous editing of the Hawaiian words and place names; and to Joyce Libby, copy editor.

I am indebted to Kepā Maly for his scholarship and assistance on Isaac Kihe and the legends of Kekaha, and to artist Herb Kane, who has immortalized Ka'ūpūlehu in his paintings. For the use of his Annie 'Una photo, a resounding mahalo to Norman Carlson. Thank you also to Haunani Apoliona for so kindly allowing us to use her lyrics from "Kukui'ohiwai," and to Barbara and Garner Anthony of Hualalai Ranch and Fred Duerr of the Kona Village Resort for their colorful reminiscences on Ka'ūpūlehu. For her personal and professional support throughout, I thank Sheila Donnelly. I also thank Laura Carter Schuster, David Clague, and Jim Kauahikaua for so generously contributing their expertise.

Special thanks go to Franco Salmoiraghi for his photographs, to Barbara Pope and her staff for the book's design, and to Kim Richards, Jeff Mongan, Roger Harris, Sam Ainslie, and the staff of the Hualalai Development Company. To Heather Cole and Jim Preskitt especially, who bore the day-to-day burdens of this project with unfailing grace, may I convey my deepest appreciation and my fervent hope: that the rewards of this book will surpass its challenges, and that the fortitude and spirit of Kekaha will endure through these changing times.

# Index

Italicized page numbers refer to illustrations.

'a'ā, 14
agriculture, 99
    traditional Hawaiian, 23
Ahua'umi *heiau*, 93
*ahupua'a*, 14–17
    after *Māhele*, 75
    See also names of *ahupua'a*
'Aimakapa'a fishpond, 77
Ai'opio fishpond, 77
AIRCOA, 110
air travel, 108
'Akahi, Chiefess, 78
'Akahipu'u, 2, 50
'Akahipu'u, legend of, 57
Akiona Store, 91
Alapa'i, Chief, 68
Alhambra, Porto, 31
'Anaeho'omalu, 13, 89, 109
Anthony, Barbara Cox, 100–101
    quoted, 101
Anthony, Garner, 100–101
    quoted, 103, 109
Apoliona, Haunani, quoted, 101
"Archaeological and Historical Survey, Honokohau Area" (Emory and Soehren), 75–77
archaeological sites, 77
astronomy, Hawaiian, 93

Barnwell Hawaiian Properties, 110
Beckwith, Martha, quoted, 20
birds, native, 32, 111
    hunting of, 23–25
Bishop, Bernice Pauahi, 75, 77–78
Bishop Estate. *See* Kamehameha Schools/Bishop Estate
Boteilho, Franklin, 87, 103
boundary markers, 76–77
Brown, Francis I'i, 94

burials, ancient, 20, 26
    See also caves
business, growth of, 86

Cambridge Pacific, 110
canoes, 26
cattle
    introduction of, 86
    shipping of, 88, 90, 91
"Cave of Makalei, The" (Kihe), 56
caves, 31–32
    burial, 26, 60
    water, 32
    as water source, 55
Choris, Louis
    drawing of von Kotzebue and Kamehameha I, 72
    watercolor of Kamehameha I, 69
citizens' groups, 113
Clague, David, quoted, 38
coconut, 66
Cole, Heather, 112, 113
Cole family, 112
Commission of Boundaries (1873), 25
Cosmo World, 110
cowboys. *See paniolo*
Cox Enterprises, 108–9
Crown Lands, 75
culture, Hawaiian, 113
    See also mythology, Hawaiian

Davis, Isaac, 70–71
Dayton, Eva Kameleapililua, 6
depopulation, 81
Dillingham Investment Company, 100
diseases, Western, 73
displacement, 81
donkeys, 96
Duerr, Fred, quoted, 108

economy
    cash, 86
    traditional Hawaiian, 20
Ellis, William, quoted, 37, 41
Emory, Kenneth P., 75–77
environmental problems, 98–100, 113

*Fair American*, 70
farming. *See* agriculture
feathers, uses of, 25
fishing, 29, 81, 97
    importance of, 22-23
fishponds, 10–11, 37, 41, 50, 60, 75, 77, 88
folklore, Kekaha, 57
    See also mythology, Hawaiian
forest fires, 111, 113
Four Seasons Resort Hawaii at Hualalai, 110–11
*Fragments of Hawaiian History* (I'i), 22

game management, 99–100
    See also goats
Giffin, Jon R., 32
goats
    hunting of, 93, 99–100
    introduction of, 86
    raising of, 96
Gourley, Richard, 102
Government Lands, 75

Haelohi'u *ahupua'a*, 75
Hainoa, 13, 16–17, 17
*halapepe*, 92, 94
Handy, Elizabeth Reen, quoted, 32
Handy, E. S. Craighill, quoted, 32
Harris, Roger, 113
Hawai'i, Kingdom of, 71–79
    coat of arms, 71, 74
    overthrow of, 79

Hawai'i, Republic of, 79
*Hawaiian Mythology* (Beckwith), 20
Hawaiian Volcano Observatory, 38
Hawai'i Island, rivalry with Maui, 65–68
Hawai'i-loa, in Hawaiian mythology, 13
Henehene, *84*
Hi'iakaikapoliopele, 49
Hilo, chiefs of, 67–68
Hina, 17
Hinakapo'ula cone, 38
Hind, Hannah, 94
Hind, Robert, 81, 88
Hōlualoa, 88
homesteading, 79–81
Honokōhau, 13, 75–77, *106–7*
Hopula'au, Luka, *4*, 87
horses, introduction of, 86
Hualalai, in Hawaiian mythology, 13
Hualalai Development Corporation, 103, 108, 111, 113
Hualalai Golf Club, 111
Hualalai Land Corporation, 109
Hualalai Ranch, *82–83*, 100–101
Hualalai village, 111
Hualalai volcano, 13–14, *14–15*, 33
  eruption of 1800–1801, 14, 35–38, 45, *46*, 50
  eruption of 1929, 33
  slopes of, *33*, 45, 113
  summit area, *14–15*, 17
  upper slopes, *18*, *19*
Hu'ehu'e, 45, 92
Hu'ehu'e eruption. *See* Hualalai volcano
Hu'ehu'e Ranch, 85–88, 92

IDG, 110
I'i, John Papa, quoted, 22, 60
implements, wooden, *68*
*Indigenous Trees of the Hawaiian Islands* (Rock), 98
Island Copra and Trading Company, 107

Isutani, Minoru, 110

Jackson, Johnno, 103, 107–8

Ka'ahumanu, Queen, 74
Kaakua, J. H., quoted, 41
*Ka Hae Hawaii* (Kaakua), 41
Kahekili, Chief, 60, 69
Kahinihini'ula pool, 77
*Ka Hoku O Hawaii* (Kihe), 20, 55, 57
Kahuā Ranch, 87
Kahuwai Bay, 26, *30*, *33*, 96, 108
Kailua, 75
Kailua Bay, *90*, *91*
Kainaliu, 100
Kaiwiopele, 50
Kajima Corporation, 111
Kalaemanō, 31, *96–97*
Kalākaua, King David, 75, 92
  quoted, 45, 49
Kalani, Chiefess Kumukea, 54
Kalaniana'ole, Prince Jonah Kūhiō, 92
Kalani'ōpu'u, Chief, 69
Kalaoa, 79
Kaloko, 75, 77, 87
  fishponds at, 60, 88
Kalola, 60
Kamakau, Samuel, quoted, 22, 37–38, 45, 46, 60, 65, 68–69, 71, 73, 108
Kamalālāwalu, tale of, 65–67
Kamanawa, Chief, 73–74
Kame'eiamoku, Chief, 25, *70*, 70, 71, 73–74
Kame'eleihiwa, Lilikalā, quoted, 73
Kāmeha'ikana, 37, 50, 52
Kamehameha I, 22, *46*, *69*, *72*
  burial cave of, 60
  offering to Pele, 38, 45
  return to Hawai'i island (1812), 22
  unification of islands, 69–71
Kamehameha II (Liholiho), 74

Kamehameha III (Kauikeaouli), *74*, 74–75
Kamehameha V (Lot Kapuāiwa), *74*, 75
Kamehameha Schools/Bishop Estate, 75, 78, 87–88, 103, 109, 111
Kāne, 54–55
Kane, Herb Kawainui
  painting by, *46*, *70*
  quoted, 71
Kapalaoa, 79–81
*Kapalaoa Homestead Life* (Kimura), 79
Kapi'olani, Queen, 87
Kapo'ikai pond, 96
Kauahikaua, Jim, quoted, 38
Ka'ū district, 65
*kauila* wood, *68*
Kaulana, 79
Ka'ūpūlehu, 17, 35, 52, 54, 70, 75, 87, 103
  development in, 110–11
  petroglyphs at, *64–65*
  shoreline of, *5*, *12–13*
Ka'ūpūlehu village, 26, *27*
Kawahaopele, 50
Kawaihae, 109
Kawaihae Bay, 65
Kawaihae Pier, *91*
Keāhole Airport (Kona), 109
Keāhole Point, 37, 45, 52
Keakealani, David, *84*
Keakealani, Robert, 26, *29*, 35, 52, 81, *84*, *90*, 90–91, *91*
Keakealani, Shirleyann, *28*
Kealalio, Mrs. Joseph, *51*
Keauhou, 74
Ke'elikōlani, Ruth, *75*, 77
Kekaha, 13
  *ahupua'a* of, *24*
  chiefly rivalry over, 67–69
  *See also place names*
Kekaulike, Chief, 68

Keōua, Chief, 60
Kihe, J.W.H. Isaac, 50, *51*, 55–57, 77, 79
    quoted, 20
Kihe, Kaimu, *51*
Kīholo, 88, 96
    fishpond, 41, 75
    ruins at, *40*
    shoreline, *66*
Kīholo Bay, 35, *39*, 60
Kimura, Larry, quoted, 79, 81
Kipikane, Rachel, 87
*kipuka*, 20, 41
Kīwalao, Chief, 69
Kohala district, 65
Kohanaiki, 75
Kona, 65
    *ali'i* of, 67–68
*Kona Legends* (Maguire), 14, 37, 50, 57
Kona petitions
    of 1845, 74
    of late 1800s, *78*, 78–79
"Kona uncles," 73
Kona Village Associates, 110
Kona Village Resort, 26, 29, 31, 52, *54*, 103, 107, 110
Kotzebue, Lieutenant Otto von, *72*
Kū, 17, 19
Kū'ili, *48–49*, 49–50
Kūki'o, *6*, 79, *80*, 88
Kūki'o Beach, 55
Kukui'ohiwai residence, 2, 25, 100, *101*
*kūpuna*, role of, 81
Ku'uali'i fishpond, *10–11*

Laehou, 41
Land Act of 1895, 79
Land Commission, establishment of, 73
land development, 107–11
    *See also* Kona Village Resort
land division. *See ahupua'a; Māhele*
Land Division of 1848. *See Māhele*

land management, Hawaiian system of, 14–17, 25
land ownership
    for *ali'i*, 74–79
    for commoners, 75, 78–79
    *See also Māhele*
lava, 14, 22
lava flow, *12–13*, *36–37*, 89
    as boundary marker, 25
    Ka'ūpūlehu flow, 38–39
lava tubes, 32
    as water source, 31, 55
*Legends and Myths of Hawaii* (Kalākaua), 45
*lehua*, 19
Lightner, Leina'ala, *28*
    quoted, 29, 31–35, 52, 90
Lili'uokalani, Queen, signature of, *92*
Loando, Gilbert, *102*
Lono, 17
*Loulu* palm, *23*
Low, Eben, 88, 90
Luahinewai pond, *1*, 60, *61*

Maguire, Aileen, *92*, *93*, 101
Maguire, Eliza D., 50, 59
    photograph by, *35*
    quoted, 14, 37, 52, 57
Maguire, John Avery, 4, 50, 87, *93*, *96–97*, 98, 101
Mahai'ula, 37, 79
Mahai'ula Bay, 45, 52
*Māhele* (1848), 25, 67, 73–75
Maka'ai, Joseph, 26, *27*, 29, 31, 35, 52, 90–91, 96
    quoted, 22–23, 41, 57–59
*Makahiki* festival, 17
Makalawena *ahupua'a*, 78
Makalawena trail, *21*
Makalawena village, 22, 25, 31, 96
    destruction of, 33
Mākālei cave, 31, 55–57
Maly, Kepā, 77
    quoted, 20, 55–56
Māmalahoa Highway, 37

Manini'ōwali, legend of, 58–60
Manini'ōwali beach, *58*, 60
Manuahi village, 50, 52
Maui, rivalry with Hawai'i Island, 65–68
Mauna Kea, 9, *14–15*
Mauna Kea Beach Hotel, 109
Mauna Lani Resort, 109
Mauna Loa, *14–15*
    eruption of 1859, 14, 35, 39, 41
McIntosh, Bob, 109
*menehune*, 57
Metcalfe, Simon, 70–71
Metcalfe, Thomas, 70
migration, 81
missionaries, arrival of, 73
*māmane*, 99
modernization, 81
mythology, Hawaiian, 49–50
    *See also* names of gods
*Myths and Legends of Hawaii* (Westervelt), 49

*Nā Paniolo o Hawai'i* (Strazar), 86
Nāpu'u, 13
*Native Land and Foreign Desires* (Kame'eleihiwa), 73
*Native Planters in Old Hawaii* (Handy and Handy), 32
Nawahine, *16–17*
Newell Bohnett, 100
North Kona district, 13

obsidian, use in tools, 89
*'ōhelo*, *44–45*, 45
*'ōhi'a*, *18–19*
Ohira, Agnes Hale'ama'u, quoted, 96
olivine, in volcanic nodules, *33*
Olowalu Massacre, 70
'O'oma, 74, 79
'Owē'owē, 20, 41, 113

Pā'aiea fishpond, 37, 50
*pāhoehoe*, 14, 22, *35*

*paniolo*, 34, 82–83, 87, 90–92, *91*, 102, *105*
Paris, Billy, *34*, 88
    quoted, 22, 32, 35, 52–54, 90–91, 94, 99–100
Parker, Eva, *95*
Parker, John Palmer, 87
Parker, Pānānā, *88*
Parker, Sam, 88
Parker Ranch, 87
Pele, 14, 37–38, 45–50
petroglyphs, *64–65*
PIA-Kona, 113
*Place Names of Hawaii*, quoted, 50
plants, alien, 98–99, 113
plants, native, 17, 98–99, 113
    protection of, 113
    uses of, 23, 26, 45, 67, 92–94, 98
    *See also* names of plants
*pōhaku*, *12–13*
ponds, *104–5*
    anchialine, 29, *55*, 60, *77*
    *See also* fishponds
Poʻopoʻomino, 59
Potomac Investment Associates, 110
Princess Hotels, 110
Puhiapele, *42–43*, 47
Puhiapele cone, *36–37*
Pukui, Mary Kawena, 41
Punihaole, Robert, quoted, 31
Purdy, James N., 79
Puʻuanahulu, 26, *28*, 81, 88, *89*, 96
Puʻuanahulu School, 94
Puʻukoholā Heiau, 60, *62–63*
Puʻuwaʻawaʻa, 32, *89*, 96
Puʻuwaʻawaʻa *ahupuaʻa*, 75
Puʻuwaʻawaʻa Ranch, 22, 26, 35, 81, *84*, 85–86, 88–91
Puʻuwaʻawaʻa Wildlife Sanctuary, 100, 111

Queen Kaʻahumanu Highway, 109

ranching, 73, 81, 101–3
    rise of, 86–87
religion, traditional Hawaiian, 73
    overthrow of, 74
    *See also* mythology, Hawaiian
Rock, Joseph F., quoted, 98
*Ruling Chiefs of Hawaii* (Kamakau), 22, 65–67, 71

salt, 20
    harvesting, 31
    importance of, 29–31
Schuster, Laura Carter, 77
    quoted, 41
Sexton, Lloyd, painting by, *106–7*
Seymour, Sadie, 94
Seymour, Scott, quoted, 92
sheep, introduction of, 86
Sheraton Royal Waikoloan, 109
Signal Oil and Gas, 108–9
social life, 92–94
Soehren, Lloyd J., 75–77
South Kohala district, 87
Springer, Hannah Kihalani, *2*, *6*, 23
    quoted, 25–26, 31, 33, 60, 86, 88, 92, 97, 98, 100
Springer, Pilipo, painting by, *94*
springs, *54*
    importance of, 31–32
Stemmermann, Lani, 6
Stillman, Arthur J., 87, 101
Stillman, Thelma, 25
Stillman Trust, 100
stone mounds, as boundary markers, *76–77*
Strazar, Marie D., quoted, 86

Tomich, Kekaulike Prosper, *6*, *101*
Tomich, Michael, *97*, *101*
Tomich, Thelma Kihalani, *6*, *101*
trade, 20, 22–23, 73, 85
trails, *ma uka—ma kai*, 20, *21*, 85, 94, 96–97
    historic, 38–41
travel, 85, 96–97
    *See also* air travel; trails
tsunami
    of 1946, 33, 96
    of 1960, 35

*uhiuhi*, 99
*ʻulu*, *55*
Uluweuweu Bay, 59
ʻUmialiloa, Chief, 20–22
ʻUna, Annie Punihaole, 31, *95*, *97*, 109

Vancouver, Captain George, 73, 86
*Voyagers* (Kane), 71

Waiaelepi, 31
Waiakauhi, 29, *57*, *104–5*
Waiokāne spring, *50*, 31, 54, *55*
Waiulu, 20
water
    drinking, 31–32, 55
    importance of, 13, 22, 31, 54–57, 107–8
Westervelt, W. D., quoted, 49
whaling ships, arrival of, 73
*wiliwili*, 98
winds, names for, 85
woodworking, 18, 68, 98, 111

Young, John, 71, *71*

## Map Labels

**Regions / Ahupuaʻa:**
- Kaʻūpūlehu Sea Fishery
- KA'ŪPŪLEHU
- PUʻUWAʻAWAʻA
- KŪKIʻO 1
- KŪKIʻO 2
- KAʻŪPŪLEHU FLOW
- FLOW OF 1801

**Place names / Features:**
- Kalaemanō
- Pōhakuokahae
- Government Land
- Pāhoehoe & old ʻAʻā
- Keahukaupuaʻa
- Kahuwai Bay
- waterhole
- Kailua – Kawaihae Road
- Kalaeʻokumukēhu
- Pāhoehoe & old ʻAʻā
- Kīholo Trail
- rocky pasture
- ʻOwēʻowē
- ʻElama & Kauila
- pasture
- grasslands
- Puʻukolekole
- ʻElama & Kauila Old ʻAʻā
- pasture
- ʻŌhiʻa
- to Kūkiʻo Beach
- Puʻupoʻopoʻomino
- trail
- Puʻumauʻu
- Pāhoehoe & old ʻAʻā
- Mountain Cabin Road
- ʻŌhiʻa & Fern
- Mūheʻenui
- Government Land
- Puʻunāhāhā
- mixed forest
- pasture
- Puʻualauʻawa
- Old ʻAʻā
- rocky pasture
- Puhiapele
- Kileo
- scattered ʻŌhiʻa & Fern
- Puʻumoanuiahea
- ʻAkahipuʻu
- Puʻuʻio
- Main Government Road
- ʻŌhiʻa